Management and Worker
The Japanese Solution

JAMES C. ABEGGLEN

Management
and
Worker

The Japanese Solution

JAMES C. ABEGGLEN

PUBLISHED BY

SOPHIA UNIVERSITY TOKYO

IN COOPERATION WITH

KODANSHA INTERNATIONAL LTD.

TOKYO, JAPAN & NEW YORK, U.S.A.

Published by
SOPHIA UNIVERSITY
7 Kioichō, Chiyoda-ku
Tokyo 102
in cooperation with
KODANSHA INTERNATIONAL LTD.
2-12-21 Otowa, Bunkyo-ku, Tokyo 112
and
KODANSHA INTERNATIONAL/USA, LTD.
Harper & Row Building
10 East 53rd Street
New York,
New York 10022
U.S.A.

World distribution rights: Kodansha International Ltd.
Distributed in Continental Europe by Boxerbooks, Inc., Zurich; in
Canada by Fitzhenry & Whiteside Limited, Ontario; and in the Far
East by Japan Publications Trading Co., P.O. Box 5030 Tokyo
International, Tokyo.

Library of Congress Catalog Card No. 72-96130
ISBN 0-87011-199-x
JBC 3033-783921-2361
First Printing, 1973

Printed in Japan

CONTENTS

LIST OF EXHIBITS

INTRODUCTION

THE REPUBLICATION in an updated version of this post–World War II classic is a most welcome event. It is amazing that this book—written in 1956 and published in 1958 as *The Japanese Factory*—can now be offered to readers with only minor additions and deletions. Although much has happened in the last sixteen years, especially in the Japanese economy, the core of this study has lost none of its interest or validity.

Since I have known the author for about twenty years—we were fellow sufferers in elementary Japanese at Harvard in 1954—it may be fitting for me to say something about him. I am especially inclined to do so because the kind of information provided on the inside of a book jacket tells far too little. Abegglen has impeccable academic credentials: Ph.D. in Social Sciences from the University of Chicago (1954), two books on American business co-authored with W. L. Warner, an assistant professorship at M.I.T. (1956–1957), etc. But he never really had patience for or with the academic world, and inevitably his interests led him into the faster-moving and more innovative realm of consulting. At present, Abegglen is Vice President of the Boston Consulting Group, an organization that has come to occupy a unique position in Japanese-American economic relations. Its services are eagerly sought by business and government on both sides of the Pacific; and BCG research also has the respect of the academic community. All of this is relevant, because *The Japanese Factory* and its successor volume *Management and Worker: The Japanese Solution* bear the stamp of a man who has been in the plants, who has talked with workers on the shop floor, and who has visited Ginza bars in the evening with the executives.

Today, when many Westerners look at Japan's recent achievements with awe, admiration, and sometimes fear, I suspect that the tone of Abegglen's book will be greeted with broad approval. He has a sympathetic understanding of Japanese practices; he praises the efficiencies of the system; he cautions against underestimating its complexities. In a word, he displays a healthy cultural relativism that recognizes the possibility of there being more than one way of organizing a labor force—and *our* way is not necessarily the best. Of course, today this sounds fairly tame, but again we should remember the relatively venerable age of this book. It is proof of Abegglen's sensitivity and understanding that he resisted the temptation to preach a Western gospel to the Japanese in the 1950's, for it was common practice at that time.

I have always believed that *The Japanese Factory* has been popular for the wrong reasons. Since the new version will undoubtedly reach an even wider readership, I would like to take this opportunity to spell out the "right" reasons—from my point of view. I think that the book has been popular because of the contrast with a much unhappier situation prevailing in the majority of Western countries. In the postwar era, the Japanese have had quite harmonious labor relations, and most manifestations of conflict—so prevalent in the United States and Western Europe—appeared to be absent. No doubt envy was a prevalent reaction in the minds of many readers— especially businessmen and perhaps even some employees and members of the younger generation anxious to avoid the "rat race." But Abegglen's researches deal with a much more fundamental point that is of growing significance in a world in which the disparities of power and technological leadership are diminishing.

Japan is the prime example in world economic history of

industrialization based on borrowed technology. This is not at all an easy process that can be dismissed by labelling it "imitation." Modern technology is capital intensive, and designed in advanced Western countries for the conditions prevailing in those countries. To introduce these techniques in Japan—an absolute necessity in order to raise levels of productivity—requires great creativity and flexibility. The Japanese had to develop a rising social capability to borrow technology, and this entailed considerable institutional innovation and adaptation, particularly the exploitation of certain traditional devices for modern purposes. The Japanese employment system certainly has traditional roots; that it was resurrected in the modern factory is a most creative adaptation that made enterprises more capable of borrowing productive technology. As Abegglen points out, with permanent employment rights, the worker has no incentive to oppose even labor-saving technological progress, while it is profitable for the employer to invest in his employees.

The lesson for the West is not specific—it has little to do with labor relations. Instead it relates to the much broader matter of flexibility and the creative change of institutions. At present, no one country is the source of all principal technology. In the near future, chances are that technical *and organizational* progress will originate in many parts of the globe—certainly in Japan. In effect, we will all have to become much more aware of and skilful at borrowing advances elsewhere. How this can be done efficiently in an atmosphere congenial to a particular culture is the main theme of this book. We should prepare ourselves to face similar—though not identical—problems.

HENRY ROSOVSKY
Harvard University
December, 1972

PREFACE

THIS BOOK presents an analysis of the Japanese employment system at three points in time—1956, 1966 and 1972, a period in which the Japanese economy grew at a rate unprecedented in history. It is at the same time an updating and partial reprinting of an earlier book entitled *The Japanese Factory: Aspects of its Social Organization.*[1]

The first part of this book is an effort to describe briefly and analyze in some detail the nature, consequences and prospects of Japan's employment system viewed in the 1970's. Part Two is reprinted from *The Japanese Factory*, a report on studies carried out in 1955 and 1956 of the organization and personnel practices of Japanese companies. Some minor deletions have been made from the original, and one chapter of the earlier book, discussing productivity, has been entirely deleted from this reprinting. Finally, a report on a study conducted in 1966 comparing that time with 1956 is included here as the final part of the book.

By way of explaining both the pattern of this book and the rationale for its preparation, the rather curious history of *The Japanese Factory* needs to be noted. The research leading to that work was in pursuit of an interest in Japan arising out

---

[1]The Free Press, Glencoe, Illinois, 1958.

of experiences during and immediately after World War II. The research findings were reported to the Ford Foundation as sponsor of a period of language study and field work. Their appearance in book form was in part happenstance and in part a result of encouragement from Professor Everett E. Hagen and other associates at the Center for International Studies of Massachusetts Institute of Technology. Publication was Center sponsored, with no real expectation of wide interest either in the West or Japan.

Quite unexpectedly, *The Japanese Factory* had a considerable impact. Two U.S. printings were exhausted rather quickly, even though the volume had no publicity and few reviews. In a mid-1960's analysis of organization literature, it was cited as among the "first generation ancestry of current work in organizational behavior," not only an "ancestral book" in the analyst's terms but "adult" (i.e., published in the late 1950's) and "more fashionable" (i.e., rather often cited in the literature).[1] An edition published in, of all places, Bombay, received critical attention in Europe.[2]

More startling, a Japanese edition entitled *Nihon no Keiei*, thanks in good part to a skilful translation by Professor Urabe Kuniyoshi of Kobe University, became both a best seller and school text in Japan.[3] Although the book dealt only generally with phenomena presumably well known to all Japanese, it went through more than twenty Japanese printings over a decade.

With all this came considerable controversy. *The Japanese Factory* was said by critics to portray the history of Japanese employment practices incorrectly—although no historical review was intended or attempted. It was said to overlook

---

[1]James G. March (editor), *Handbook of Organizations* (Chicago: Rand McNally & Company, 1965), p.x.

[2]Asia Publishing Company, Bombay, 1958.

[3]Diamondo Sha, Tokyo, 1958.

the role of small business—although the report explicitly and deliberately concentrated on large business. Again, an ideological bias toward management has been charged to the book—an issue that seems irrelevant to the question of the accuracy of the report or its analysis. More important, the analysis was said to overlook both the existence of and potential for change. The controversy continues. This fact, along with frequent requests for copies of the book, long out of print, is taken as justification for an effort to present a time perspective on and reassessment of Japan's employment system and for reprinting much of the earlier work.

This is the intellectual rationale for presenting this book. There are other and more personal reasons. First, the opportunity to observe and play some marginal part in the immense achievement of Japan over the past twenty-five years has been and remains exciting and satisfying. Even against an experience of the engagements in the Pacific, the devastation of Japan—of Tokyo, Nagoya, Osaka, and most of all Hiroshima—and the poverty of the countryside in 1945 was a shock. The brilliantly planned and executed recovery and further progression from that appalling base can only be admired. This book is an effort to record one aspect of that achievement.

A second reason is closely related to the first. More perhaps than the people of any other country, the Japanese welcome efforts to learn about their language and their society and offer the most warm hospitality and assistance to these learning efforts. There is then not only the satisfaction of attempting to understand one part of an historic achievement but also the pleasure and reward of friendship and sympathy in the effort. It seems only proper to report the results.

This book covers a period of more than fifteen years of considerable involvement with Japan, leaving aside the wartime and immediately postwar experience. A great many people have been teachers and critics over this time. Among these, Hachiya Saburo and Uchida Yukio must be noted as principals both in instruction and criticism. More as sponsors than critics, Hasegawa Norishige, Kobayashi Koji, Kitagawa Kazue, Tashiro Shigeki and the late Nabeshima Tsunatoshi, both by their own achievements and by their support, have helped make work in Japan meaningful and gratifying.

Other obligations need to be noted. Bruce D. Henderson and other associates in The Boston Consulting Group have done much to clarify and refine the analysis of the economic consequences of Japan's employment system. The Patent and Copyright Office of MIT generously offered unrestricted reprint rights to *The Japanese Factory*. Robert J. Ballon, by his interest and efforts, has some considerable responsibility for the preparation of this book.

Yet, for all of this assistance and instruction, this book is one person's effort, with personal responsibility for errors, to pay respects to the achievement of Japan.

JAMES C. ABEGGLEN
Tokyo
September, 1972

Part I

THE JAPANESE EMPLOYMENT SYSTEM IN THE 1970's

Japan's economic achievements necessarily imply a highly efficient system for the allocation of the capital and labor resources available to the economy. Yet, despite all evidence of high efficiency in economic performance, the view persists that Japan's unique approach to employment of its labor resources is ineffective, and must change to the Western pattern. In fact, the system of employment in Japan is a considerable source of strength in pursuing economic growth and well-being. Change, as it inevitably occurs, may well be in the direction of further innovations.

Part I

THE JAPANESE EMPLOYMENT
SYSTEM IN THE 1970's

THE COMPLEX interaction of tradition and very rapid change is at once the fascination and the challenge of the study of Japan. No nation in this generation has changed more swiftly; no nation retains its identity more surely. The challenge of analysis and prediction is to separate out those aspects of Japan that will continue essentially unchanged from those that will yield readily to the opportunities and pressures of the moment.

In the economic sector, the dialectic between the stable and the transitory comes into sharp focus in the field of organization, the manner in which people are brought into, trained, rewarded or punished, and related to each other in large industrial or financial organizations. Japan has a unique employment system, deriving its strength from its being based firmly on Japan's social system. Yet this employment system is subject to the massive economic changes taking place in Japan as well as to the changes in attitudes and values resulting from industrialization and affluence.

The problem in considering changes in Japan's employment system is that of understanding its bases of strength, reviewing the pressures it is under, and attempting to gauge the effects of the transition-continuity interaction. Japan is clearly in transition, and not for the first time. Yet continuity of values and behavior remains a central theme. The analysis of Japan's unique employment system, its strengths, weaknesses and the pressures on it for continuity and change provides a test case of the larger issue of continuity and change in Japanese society.

Japan again in Transition

It is evident that the early years of the 1970's mark a broad-ranging transition period for Japan and its economy. Since the end of World War II, barely a generation, the nation's unparalleled economic achievements have built the world's most effective industrial complex. Incomes and output are at European levels, an order of magnitude greater than had been thought possible in Asia. Both in trade and in politics the world will be attempting to come to terms with the Japan phenomenon for decades.

Yet this achievement by its magnitude has raised major new issues for Japan, only now becoming clear. They are essentially the issues of defining an international role. In external affairs, the passive policies the Japanese government has been following are inappropriate to its present economic strength, are not responsive to changing world power relations, and are increasingly unsatisfactory to the Japanese public. Relations with the United States, the Soviet Union and the People's Republic of China are undergoing urgent reexamination. Further, the problems involved in massive overseas capital investment and extensive foreign aid programs, unprecedented in the history of Japan or of any Asian country, are now being addressed.

Within Japan, the long-deferred needs for increased public expenditure have new and higher priorities, as the flow of new investment capital is being diverted into the social overhead sector. Along with this, during a period of slower economic growth, private capital is reexamining the directions of industrial investment over the decade. Further, a new generation of political leaders is just coming on stage, men who will seek to give political focus to the interests of the postwar, urban, industrial Japanese public.

These issues suggest very great changes indeed in Japan over the next several years, changes whose impact on the nation and the world may well be as far-reaching as the economic events of the past two decades. But these are changes in public policy and changes in resource allocation. New directions in policy can be undertaken without the society necessarily undergoing changes in its basic patterns of behavior or thinking. To what extent have more basic changes taken place in Japan over this past generation of unprecedented changes in economic circumstance? What changes might be expected in the society; what new directions are likely in the fundamental patterns of behavior and interaction?

Continuity in Change

As a point of departure in addressing these questions, it needs first to be emphasized that Japan is a non–Western society. Its history, geography, religions, language, racial composition, and political traditions are Asian, not of the West. It is the only non–Western nation to have industrialized. It is the nation of Asia that has demonstrated that the period of Western imperial ascendancy was fated to be brief, first politically and now economically. If this emphasis on Japan's Asian position and unique social traditions appears to be emphasis of a truism, let it be noted that a good deal of discussion of changes in Japan deplores this emphasis and insists on a considerable similarity between Japanese and Western society.

It can be argued that it is the underlying continuity and stability of Japanese society that has made the enormous achievements of the past generation possible. The social changes inherent in the move from per capita output of a little over $100 in 1950 to nearly $2,000 in 1970 are enormous. From famine in some regions at the war's end, rice is now in embarrassing surplus. From nearly half of the work force in agriculture, the proportion is now only 15 percent, with Japan one of the most urbanized nations in the world. The death rate has been halved, as life expectancy nears the highest levels in the world, increasing by nearly 20 years in only 20 years. Incomes in current prices have increased more than 45 times in the 23 years since 1947. As a more homely index of social change, the Ministry of Education found it necessary to increase the size of the standard school desk, since Japan's postwar children are larger than earlier generations.

Social change far less dramatic than this has played havoc with the social fabric of nations less homogeneous and less stable than Japan. In the Japanese case, these great changes have been joined with a high degree of political stability, very low rates of crime and other social pathologies, and a steadily higher national morale. Some part of this must be owed to good management; some considerable part must bespeak the strength of the society and its traditions. Far from being "a fragile blossom" as one visitor suggested, this is a strong and healthy society. Professor Nakane suggests a key to that strength:

It is in informal systems rather than in overt cultural elements that persistent factors are to be found. The informal system, the driving force of Japanese activities, is a native Japanese brew, steeped in a unique characteristic of Japanese culture. In the course of modernization Japan imported many western cultural elements, but these were and are always partial and segmentary and are never in the form of an operating system. It is like a language with its basic indigenous structure or grammar which has accumulated a heavy overlay of borrowed vocabulary; while the outlook of Japanese society has suffered drastic changes over the past hundred years, the basic social grammar has hardly been affected.[1]

The strength of the Japanese economic system similarly has derived from the fact that Japan's industrialization has taken place by the introduction of Western technology and methods into a Japanese social context. The result is a unique business system, the most effective approach to economic management the world has yet seen. In the melding of imported techniques to a Japanese context, special business practices have developed, especially in the allocation and use of human resources, in the optimal use of financial resources, and in the interrelations between government and business, that differ markedly from those in the West.[2]

Japan's Employment System

It is the employment system in Japan—the allocation and use of human resources—that is at once the most paradoxical, the most discussed, and the most liable to Western ethnocentricity in its evaluation. Paradox arises from the fact that the Japanese employment system has very considerable strengths, yet is commonly seen in the West as inefficient and virtually unworkable. Controversy stems both from arguments over the system's causes and outcomes, and from the view that it must surely change—and in the Western fashion.

It seems appropriate, as Japan undergoes still further

---

[1]Nakane Chie, *Japanese Society* (London: Weidenfeld and Nicolson, 1970), p. 149.

[2]Abegglen, James C., "The Economic Growth of Japan," *Scientific American,* Vol. 222 (March 1970).

transitions in outward manner, to reexamine the Japanese employment system and its effects, and raise again the questions of whether and when the system might change.

The main features of what will be called here Japan's employment system include in brief summary the following:

1. Recruitment of the employee is directly from school. Entrance to the work force is from the bottom of the age-ranking, and not from an open labor market.

2. Recruitment is in terms of personal qualifications, and into the work group. Employees are not hired for specific jobs, nor do they apply for specific jobs. Rather they are hired because of an expectation that additional employees will be required, and on the assumption that skills not provided by general educational background will be provided through company training. Qualifications then are intelligence, character and general acceptability as determined by personal history, academic record and company tests and interviews.

3. Employment is for the entire career of the individual. Both employer and employee assume that the employment relationship is permanent, that the company will not discharge or lay off the employee and that the employee will not change to another employer during his career.

4. Compensation depends basically and largely on length of service. Initial compensation is a function of the level of education completed; subsequent increases in compensation are a function of length of service, which in this system of course correlates directly with age.

5. The trade union bargaining unit includes all company employees, with few, if any, jurisdictional issues. The union contract is generally limited to recognition and to compensation of members, and bargaining is predictably seasonal (the "spring struggle").

These are the skeletal features of the Japanese employment system. It has associated aspects that are important and unusual but not critical to the system. There is, for example, a general practice of retirement at the age of 55 years, ameliorated by the possibility of assignment to subsidiaries and increasingly subject to experiments with a more advanced retirement age. Again, an important component of cash compensation is the bonus, negotiated with the union and loosely a function of company profitability, that is paid twice annually and is a considerable increment to base compensation. Further, a wide variety of allowances is paid to compensate for family size, hazardous work, posting to undesirable locations, and the like. And a part of the employment pattern is a general tendency to take only brief holidays, rather than following the Western pattern of extended vacation. Several of these kinds of unique patterns have important consequences, as, for example, the impact of the bonus payment system on Japan's savings rate. They may be seen, however, as marginal to the basic pattern of employment relations.

This Japanese employment pattern, emphasizing group membership rather than individual skills, involving employer and employee in a permanent and complex relationship of mutual obligation, and rewarding tenure rather than short-term performance, is consistent with and is based on very fundamental and very long continued patterns in Japanese society. It is also a very modern employment system in another sense. In its present form it has been institutionalized since the end of World War II and in that regard may be taken to be the most recent pattern of employment amongst the developed economies of the world. Again, in this regard as well as others, it is a paradoxical system, at once rooted in the social traditions of Japan and at the same time the product of recent economic history.

The Japanese employment system as described above is a

statement of the ideal type. In practice there are of course exceptions to each of its essential features. However, this summary fairly states both the norm and the general practice. Conceptually and analytically it is the norm that is critical; the exceptions comprise footnotes to the rule. Among exceptions there is some movement of younger people from small to large companies, and considerable movement of workers between smaller firms (although smaller firms follow the system as an "ideal" within their economic capability). There is some movement of specialists who are in temporary short supply between large companies. Further, large companies have some part of their labor force in the category of "temporary workers" who are, as the term implies, outside these general rules. As another exception of sorts, female workers generally leave the firm on marriage rather than remaining in the employment system.

With these caveats, the pattern of employment described above may be fairly taken to be the general pattern in large Japanese companies. The patterns described pertain to the industrial and financial institutions that dominate the resources and output of the economy. In examining the question of change in Japan's employment system, it is necessary to examine both its strengths and its weaknesses, for these will largely determine the rate and direction of change.

Motivation of the Labor Force

It is surely self-evident that, to be effective, the organization of the workplace in any society must be consistent with the underlying values and patterns of interaction in that society. Thus in a relatively individualistic society like that of the United States, where relationships have a considerable element of contract, and where economic relations in particular tend to be depersonalized, it is not surprising that the system of recruitment and compensation in companies conforms to these underlying patterns in the society. Rather clearly, if the organization of the workplace were discontinuous from and not congruent with the organization of the family, the school and other primary institutions, the workplace would not function effectively.

By the same token, to the extent that Japanese society is different from the West in values and in interaction patterns, so it would be expected that the organization of the workplace would differ. Indeed, it is reasonable to conclude that the very success of Japanese industry argues for a high degree of organizational congruence to the special features of Japanese culture. The sociological roots of Japan's employment system, and its effectiveness in motivating Japanese employees, are suggested by Nakane after reviewing Japanese family interaction:

> Another group characteristic portrayed in the Japanese household can be seen when a business enterprise is viewed as a social group. In this instance a closed social group has been organized on the basis of the 'life-time employment system' and the work made central to the employees' lives. The new employee is in just about the same position and is, in fact, received by the company in much the same spirit as if he were a newly born family member, a newly adopted son-in-law or a bride come into the husband's household....
>
> The relationship between employer and employee is not to be explained in contractual terms. The attitude of the employer is expressed by the spirit of the common saying, 'the enterprise is the people'. This affirms the belief that employer and employee are bound as one by fate in conditions which produce a tie between man and man often as firm and close as that between husband and

wife. Such a relationship is manifestly not a purely contractual one between employer and employee; the employee is already a member of his own family, and all members of his family are naturally included in the larger company 'family'.[1]

A first and most general view then of the basis for the high morale and motivation that observers commonly credit to the Japanese work force is that this motivation derives from the fact that the organization of the workplace parallels the organization of Japan's primary institutions. The company is recipient of the kind of identification and loyalty that is the basis of family organization. It is clear, too, that under these conditions the economic organization must respond reciprocally by concern for the employee's general well-being, his housing, his holidays, and such family events as marriages, births and deaths. Japanese companies do express their interest and concern through appropriate allowances, gifts and company recreation facilities.

It is also clear that, if this is the basis for the relationship, dismissal can be undertaken only in extreme cases; or if "the family" is breaking up—in the economic case, bankruptcy. Even layoff is an extreme behavior. When under pressure of the 1971 turn-down in color television demand, Hitachi determined that temporary layoffs were required (and obtained union concurrence), laid-off workers were guaranteed payment of 85 percent of their previous base wage on the first day of layoff, 90 percent the second day, and 95 percent thereafter.

The congruence with the social substrata is the basis for the employment system. This is not to say that the workplace is "one big, happy family," that all motives are benign, or

---

[1]Nakane, *op. cit.*, pp. 14–15.

that ambitious or frustrated men never look over their shoulder longingly at other employers. But consider the effects of the system on job change and on work motivation. The man joins the company fresh from school, and presumably for his career. To be available for employment elsewhere is to be branded in the eyes of most potential employers as one who has been a problem. There must be something wrong or else why is he available? Further, the rather rigid patterns of pay and of retirement allowance as well as the informal work group structure make it exceedingly difficult to fit a new man into an organization except at the bottom of the hierarchy.

In short, from the point of view of the employee his future and his family's future depend on the success of the company that now employs him. If that company prospers and grows, he will be promoted, his bonuses will wax fat, and his family's and his future is assured. If the company does badly, so does he and so do his dependents. His choices are few, and therefore, his motivation to work hard and do well by the company is correspondingly strong. (And if he was so uninformed or ill-advised as to join a declining industry such as coal mining or textiles on graduation from school, one can only be sadly sympathetic.) Under these conditions, it is not surprising that there is a high degree of identification with the company and its fortunes. Not only is there a strong social and psychological basis for the identification, but the realities of the career mightily reinforce it.

So, too, for the company. It is no small matter for a Japanese company when an employee announces his decision to leave. By so doing, he is declaring to the community that the company has not taken proper care of him, and is not meeting its obligations to its employees. Most foreign companies in Japan (they are, after all, the organizations that can offer positions to older men without necessarily upsetting their structures) have considerable experience with the very great pressures Japanese companies exert to ensure that no one leaves. The impact on the prestige of a Japanese company of a defecting employee is felt deeply since it affects the company's reputation, its ability to attract recruits, and its credibility with its present staff.

It would appear then that in a Japanese context this employment system is a powerful mechanism for motivation. It has two faces. It taps first the very basic motives involved in group-centered, non-contractual, hierarchy-oriented society. And on this base is laid an employment and compensation pattern that reinforces the identification of employer and employee. Personal success and company success become inextricably intermeshed.

Distribution of the Labor Force

Many Western observers on first view of the Japanese employment system reach the conclusion that it has substantial economic inefficiencies due to the immobility of the labor force that the system imposes. This is a simplistic view; it can more properly be argued that the system makes for an especially efficient allocation of the labor force in terms of economic growth.

Consider the question of labor cost. A well-run economy is that in which the more efficient—and therefore faster-growing —business or industry has steady cost advantage relative to the less efficient company or industry. The Japanese employment system works directly to ensure this outcome.

It has been noted that workers enter the Japanese company directly from school rather than horizontally from an open labor market. It has been further noted that their compensation is a direct function of length of service (i.e., age). Thus labor costs are directly related to the average age of the work force. It is no accident that Japan is the one country in which standard information on a company includes, along with balance sheet, shareholders and the like, the average age of work force, divided usually by male and female employees. This is critical competitive data since it indicates the labor cost levels of the company, and by comparison with other companies, competitive labor costs.

A fast-growing company or industry has some competitive advantage that causes its more rapid growth rate. It is in the economic interest of the total economy to support the fast-growth sectors. But fast growth carries with it a requirement that the labor force expand relatively rapidly. Thus the company that is growing rapidly, and for whatever reason gaining competitive advantage, is hiring large numbers of personnel directly from school.

This addition of young workers directly from school to the work force lowers the average age of the work force of the successful and growing company or industry. Thereby the average cost of labor for the company or industry is reduced. Thus, whatever the factors that were causing the company or industry to gain competitive advantage and grow more rapidly are now very much reinforced by a steady improvement in wage rates compared to a more slowly growing company or industry.

Conversely, a slow-growing company or industry, adding few if any members to its work force, is subject to a steady increase in its average wage rate as its work force ages. Whatever caused its slower growth, the result is now reinforced on the negative side by a widening cost disadvantage.

Thus, the system of recruitment and pay must be seen as highly efficient in terms of labor cost effects in reinforcing growth. It has further benefits for the growth sectors. Younger workers hired directly from school are those workers with the most recent technological training. While the work force of a slow-growing firm experiences a steady obsolescence of its skill levels, the fast-growing firm is steadily improved. New technology then is allocated to the growth sectors by this system.

These effects are not confined to the lower ranks of the work force. Since management is not recruited from outside the company, the fast-growing company with a rapidly expanding work force must place executive authority in the hands of younger management personnel. While the management of companies in the slow-growth sectors ages therefore, and presumably becomes less aggressive and risk-taking, management of companies in the fast-growth sectors is placed in the hands of younger, probably more aggressive, leaders.

A further factor operates to reinforce the tendency of this system to foster growth in the economy. When the choice of company is a career choice, and essentially irrevocable, a man is likely to be thoughtful indeed in deciding which company he will join. In fact, in Japan he will depend heavily on the advice of senior advisors, especially teachers, friends and family, to ensure that his decision is sound and well based. To the extent that he is perceptive and careful in his decision, he will seek to join a firm and an industry that has the widest choice of the best men in its recruiting, the process again reinforcing the successful firm and working against the interests of the less successful firm.

Thus, this system of employment has the enormous advantage of shifting the lowest cost, most recently trained part of the labor force to the most modern and most rapidly growing sectors of the economy. It ensures younger management in the more rapidly growing sectors. And the reverse of the coin is the disadvantage at which it places the slower-growing sectors, those firms or industries that need to be phased out if the economy is to continue to grow.

In the conventional Western view of Japan's employment system it prevents the free operation of market forces in allocating labor supply. It is clear, however, that this is a simplistic view that fails to note the dynamics of the system in fostering growth and competitive advantage. This conventional view also fails to take into account the fact that while mobility of labor between large firms is in fact very much limited, mobility within the firm is encouraged by this employment system. As the size of the efficient corporate unit increases, this capacity for intrafirm mobility goes far to balance whatever disadvantages may result from lack of interfirm mobility.

Mobility from job to job in the firm is possible in the Japanese case both from the fact that the worker has no critical reason to object to reassignment and that management has a considerable incentive to provide training for a new position. From the employee's point of view, his tenure is assured, and his income based primarily on length of service. A move from one job to another within the firm then threatens neither compensation nor employment. For the company, the worker is a fixed cost and continued obligation; since employment change is rare, retraining does not run the risk of the worker taking his new skills elsewhere for other employment as it does in the West. Finally, as discussed further below, the union is not a skill union, nor does the union contract specify job content, and thus the labor contract is no obstacle to mobility from one job to another.

The positive effects of this intrafirm mobility should not be minimized. The ability to deploy the work force within the company to meet requirements no doubt helps explain the ability of Japanese companies to meet tight construction schedules by redeploying engineers as needed on projects, or, as another example, the success of Japan's shipbuilding industry where the rigidities of job definitions and assignments have greatly handicapped British and U.S. companies competitively.

Stability of Labor Relations

The pattern of relations between the company and trade union that has developed in Japan is an important and generally underestimated factor in explaining the economy's competitive strength. Trade unions are a powerful force in Japan, and studies of workers' attitudes indicate that the Japanese employee looks on his union as a critical check against an otherwise excessively powerful management. At the same time, the pattern of labor relations that has developed has avoided the rigidities in work force management and has worked to minimize the enormous economic costs of strikes that have proved so devastating to the economies of Europe and the United States.

The Japanese labor force is unionized to the same extent as is the case in the West. About 30 percent of the labor force are union members, and this proportion has held quite steady for a number of years. The basic unit of unionization is the "enterprise union," which takes in as members all the employees of the company, whatever their particular job. The labor contract deals primarily with union recognition and with compensation; it does not cover such matters as job content, speed of the assembly line and the like as in the West. Negotiation is essentially over compensation. These "enterprise unions" are in turn affiliated generally to industry-wide federations which in turn are members of one of the several nationwide federations. These are essentially politically preoccupied, the largest the chief support of Japan's Peking-oriented Socialist Party.

Parallels to the basic employment system of this pattern of union relations are clear, and inevitable. The employment pattern emphasizes company membership rather than occupation or skill identification. No surprise then that craft or skill unions are virtually unknown. The bargaining unit takes in all employees of the company, keeping intact even in the

context of union relations the concept of company membership and identification. The integrity of the company unit is
maintained despite the identification of the union with
federations whose activities extend beyond the company. The
union serves its purpose as a check on management that otherwise might exploit the work force, but does so in a way consistent with the basic pattern of Japan's employment system.

The stability of labor relations that this system provides
must be seen as a principal source of competitive advantage of
Japanese firms in world competition. It makes possible flexible
use of the labor force and rapid introduction of new technology while minimizing the costs to the economy of work
stoppages. Looking first at the work stoppage issue, without
compromising the union as a representative of the worker in
disputes with management, the Japanese approach to union-
company relations reduces the incidence of strikes, limits their
duration and, by their seasonal predictability, very much reduces their competitive costs.

The direct cost of strikes in Japan has in recent years been
about one-seventieth the cost of strikes in the United States.
That is, man-hours lost to strikes, multiplied by cost per man-
hour, was seventy times greater in the U.S. case. Note that
this is an absolutely minimum estimate of the cost of labor
disputes. There is in addition the cost to the economy of man-
hours lost as a result of layoffs and production stoppages in
supplier firms when buyer firms are struck, and the cost of
lack of product. The costs of a prolonged strike in General
Motors or General Electric go far beyond the direct man-
hours lost by strike in those firms, owing to the effects on sup-
pliers and customers.

Further, the costs of strikes in the West are greater than in
Japan because of the incidence in the West of strikes in which
a few workers in a skill union are able to close down production
for the company as a whole. These considerable effects are not

reflected in the simple calculation of man-hours lost due to strikes. Finally, the unpredictability of strikes in the West raises considerably their economic cost. Stockpiling of inventories in anticipation of strikes is one example. Lost customers to international competitors is another. Consider the cost to Japan, supplying world customers through a ten-thousand-mile pipeline, if assurance of supply to customers was substantially affected by the likelihood of unpredictable supply stoppage.

A precise calculation of the difference in economic cost of the differing systems of labor relations probably cannot be made. Let it only then be concluded that Japan realizes a very large advantage from its system of labor relations. These derive from three basic factors.

First, the issue of jurisdictional disputes and of separate negotiations with several bargaining entities does not arise in the Japanese case. Management deals with a single bargaining entity, and is not subject to the hazard of a small group in the work force holding the entire company to ransom to achieve its bargaining objectives. This carries with it the hazard that the single bargaining entity has massive power. Just as one union cannot take advantage of others in negotiations, so management in Japan cannot set one union against another. What limits the potentially enormous power of the single bargaining unit?

Here we must refer again to the system of career employment. If the worker's well-being and that of his family depend very heavily on the well-being of the company as a whole, and if their future and the company's future are tightly interrelated, there is then a sharp limit to the extent to which he, or he and his fellows in the union, is prepared to damage the company. Bearing in mind the fact that Japanese companies make heavy use of debt in their financing and thus have a very limited cash position, and noting also that competition for market share in Japan is very strong, it is clear that the consequences of an extended strike for a Japanese company would be devastating. Granted it does General Motors no good to take a three-month strike, the average Japanese company could not withstand a strike of far less duration. The company would be destroyed. And thereby the cost to the worker would be equally disastrous.

Under these conditions, it is not surprising that strikes tend to be during early morning hours, or at lunch hour, or at five o'clock. Or for a day. Not to say that these are not meaningful as a threat, and as a reminder to management of the union's power. They are a real statement of power relations, but limited in their cost to the company and to the economy.

Note, too, that under the Japanese system of employment there is not the same separation of interest as in the U.S. or European case. In Western terms, there are "parties to the dispute," adversaries whose interests and objectives are quite distinct. But this distinction of parties to the dispute is much less clear when the enterprise union which takes in all of the employees of the company, who expect to spend their careers in the company, deals with the management of that company in a dispute. Their interests are not separate. Thus it is not surprising that a company doing poorly in a given year can ask for understanding in wage negotiations for that year with the promise that the shortfall in wage increase will be made up for in a year or two when the company is doing better. The work force will be there in a year or two, and the promise is a meaningful one.

Finally, the predictability of strikes in Japan needs to be noted to appreciate fully their limited economic cost. A pattern has developed whereby wage disputes, or more precisely the issue of annual increases in compensation for the work force, come into focus in the spring of the year, the so-called "spring struggle." Some 90 percent of the limited man-hours lost to strikes takes place in April. Thus both the company and its customers can anticipate supply interruptions and adjust inventories accordingly. Again, this is an economic advantage difficult to measure but undoubtedly an important factor in minimizing the economic cost of labor disputes.

It should be noted that the unions generally support and are an important reinforcement to the present system of employment. A system of compensation based on seniority, and a system of employment tenure, is no less attractive to Japanese unions than to unions elsewhere in the world. Thus the union in Japan, far from being a force for change in employment practices, is in fact a considerable factor in maintaining the basic characteristics of the employment system.

Because union membership is undifferentiated by skills, it is also the case that the union contract is no barrier to job flexibility. In the West, the union contract serves to maintain the system of skills existing at a given moment in order to preserve the jobs of union members. This obviously introduces rigidity in work assignment and resistance to technological change. Since union membership in Japan is undifferentiated by job, the union contract is no obstacle to work force mobility from job to job, nor is it a barrier to the introduction of new technology that might change job content.

In summary, labor relations in Japan have taken a quite different pattern than in the West. The Japanese pattern of trade union relations is, inevitably, consistent with the overall employment system. The consequences of this pattern are to Japan's very considerable economic advantage.

Introduction of New Technology

In 1950 the per capita output of the Japanese economy was at about the level of most of Southeast Asia today, a little over $100. Over the next two decades output increased almost 20 times to nearly $2,000, or the level of Western Europe. This change is both a measure of the magnitude of Japan's economic achievement and also an index of the extent of technological change that has taken place in the Japanese economy. Clearly, this enormous economic growth requires huge inputs of technology into the workplace. One measure of the amount of technology introduced is the fact that more than 15,000 contracts were entered into by Japanese companies with Western firms over the 1950–1970 period for the purchase of Western technology.

Each of these technological inputs, whether from foreign or domestic sources, carries with it a change in nature of the job, some amount of adjustment in the workplace, as the product or the process of production changes to introduce new technology. Since each of these inputs requires job change, this long sustained rate of technological change argues that the Japanese employment system must be highly flexible. Each change in product or process requires work force adjustment. The skill content of a given job must change; some jobs inevitably are wiped out by new technology; some are downgraded; new skill requirements are introduced; each introduction of technology is a threat to the existing system of work relations. It is not surprising then that in the West there is a long history of resistance to new technology; it is fair to say that the rate of technological change experienced by Japan could not be achieved in Great Britain or the United States because of the strain this change would place on employee and trade union relations. How has the Japanese company been able to introduce such rapid technological change without destructive consequences for employee relations?

Again reference to the system of employment is necessary. If employment is "permanent," then new technology does not threaten the employment of the worker. He will retain his employment in any event, even if the new product or process wipes out his particular job. In fact, the new product or process does not even threaten his level of compensation. He is paid basically according to seniority, and therefore the fact that a particular job is displaced technologically is not a threat to income. Thus, new technology is no threat. Indeed, if the technology is in fact useful competitively, and thereby improves the position of the company, it is to the worker's advantage that it be introduced since as the company benefits, so will he in the form of more rapid advancement, larger bonuses from increased profits, increased job security, and enlarged prestige from company success. In short, new technology in the Japanese system brings with it no negative results; rather, to the extent that it is effective, the introduction of new technology can have only positive benefits.

In the West, the Luddite tradition is never far from the surface. New technologies are a menace. They displace particular jobs, obsolete present skills, and can only be a threat to the work force. This fact is embodied in the trade union agreements of the West in which job content is specified and job changes require renegotiation of contractual commitments. The Japanese company is freed of these constraints on the introduction of new technology; indeed, the nature of the employment relationship is such that new technology, if it is in fact productive, can only be welcomed by the work force as a benefit. When the question is argued as to whether the Japanese economy can keep pace with Western technological developments, this fact needs to be kept in mind. There is an inherent Japanese advantage, under present conditions, in the race for commercial application of new technology.

In summary then, the Japanese employment system is an efficient one, a system that makes possible unusually full and efficient use of the labor resources of the economy. It provides for a high level of worker motivation and involvement. It makes possible a highly effective distribution of the work force into those sectors of the economy where advantage is sought in terms of growth and international competitive capability. A high potential for intrafirm mobility from one job to another helps compensate for diminished interfirm mobility. It is a system that goes far to solve the problem of the terrible economic costs of trade unions to Western economies while retaining their critical advantage. It is, finally, a system that makes possible a high rate of technological change.

The Japanese employment system has on occasion been described in the West as "uneconomic." Clearly this is not true. Japanese observers have on occasion suggested that it is somehow "feudal." Clearly this characterization is irrelevant, not to say nonsensical. This is an employment system very well adapted indeed to the requirements both of Japanese society and of modern industry.

Putting to one side these kinds of general and pejorative criticisms of the system, it must be said that there is a considerable view both in academic and business discussions that Japanese employment practices are inefficient and need to be changed—"modernized," as the usual phrase goes. While little or no concrete evidence is at hand of change in the system, like any institutional pattern in a rapidly shifting society the employment system developed in Japan has disadvantages and weaknesses. In assessing the question of the rate and direction of probable change it is first necessary to examine in some detail the problems, weaknesses and disadvantages of the Japanese employment system. While the Japanese employment system provides very considerable economic advantages, it involves some substantial disadvantages as well.

Lack of Labor Mobility

The difficulties for the economy that might arise from the reduced labor mobility in this employment system are much mitigated by the intrafirm mobility noted earlier. The employment system described here principally characterizes large companies, those employing thousands of workers. Mobility in the smaller business sector is more common. This makes small businesses less desirable employers, not only for reasons of prestige but also and more urgently for reasons of lack of job security.

For the individual company, the immobility of the system poses some real problems. There is first of all an overstaffing required in consequence of the difficulty of hiring from outside the company when additional personnel are needed. It is self-evident that in this system a company that expects continued growth must hire from the universities and high schools not the number of men needed at the time of hiring, but rather the number of men that are likely to be needed to fill positions in the future. As a result, the large company has on hand a pool of younger, university-graduated staff which tends not to be drawn into meaningful activity for several years after employment.

This real cost disadvantage should not be exaggerated. Since newly hired men are low salaried, the costs involved are not large. Further, the availability of these young men means that Japanese companies are able to do, and commonly do, an amount of staff work in terms of project planning and market research that is prodigious by Western standards. Still, this is a real cost disadvantage of the system. This phenomenon also results in a high rate of disaffection among these frustrated young men, who are given as a result to complaining of the lack of opportunity and the ponderous nature of the hierarchy. No doubt it is these complaints, which trail off as these men are drawn into more significant jobs with time, that help give rise to the recurrent view that "the system is changing," and that "young people are different."

A further disadvantage of the system in terms of employment costs is the difficulty of removing from the payroll employees of demonstrated incompetence. As an example, the personnel department of a major steel complex recently identified some 50 employees who for reason of physical or mental disability were unable to perform usefully on any job. The suggestion was made to the senior manager of the complex that these people be discharged. The suggestion was rejected on the classic grounds that the company had an obligation to continue the employment of these people, especially in view of Japan's generally poor provisions for social welfare.

It is interesting to speculate on the relative costs to the total economy of welfare programs provided by private corporations compared with governments. The provisions for housing, retirement and income security by the large Japanese corporation are an alternative to government welfare programs. One might guess that they are more efficiently provided by the corporation.

These costs to the individual company of "permanent employment" must in competitive international terms be set off against the costs in Western employment systems of fairly high turnover of personnel. The frictional costs of repeated recruiting and training of replacement personnel certainly balance in some degree the costs of retaining less than competent individuals and of temporary overstaffing.

A more substantial problem arising from the limitations on labor mobility has to do with technology. As the Japanese company seeks to enter a new field in which technical skills are required which are not available within the company, it clearly encounters a major obstacle from its difficulties in recruiting those new skills. There is some reason to believe this has been a disadvantage to Japanese firms in the computer area, where technology has been changing very rapidly.

Dependence on Growth

Can this system of employment survive a long-sustained period of slow economic growth? If the work force cannot be reduced in size, abrupt downturns in demand can have a devastating effect on costs. If compensation increases steadily with seniority, a continued flatness in demand will result in steady and inexorable cost increases. Given Japan's economic performance, the question has no historical answer. What may be said, however, is that in any economy at any time, barring an improbable and disastrous long-continued depression, some companies and sectors are growing, while others are not. It was noted above that the Japanese employment system works to the considerable competitive advantage of growth companies and industries. It perhaps needs to be more explicitly pointed out that the effects of the system on slow growth firms and industries are sharply negative. Costs rise steadily, work force quality erodes, these and other factors limit access to bank and equity funding, and a downward, nearly irreversible spiral sets in.

In terms of an economy that seeks to continue to grow and thereby to continue to elevate the living standards of its people, the consequences of this growth-linked system can only be beneficial. Continued growth, as Japanese policy explicitly recognizes, requires that resources of both capital and labor be steadily shifted and reallocated to higher technology growth sectors. To the extent that the employment system reinforces this policy, the results can only be welcomed, for all of the stress that the shift of resources out of a company or industry may occasion.

High Fixed Costs

A clear consequence of the Japanese employment system is

its impact on production and pricing policy. Labor costs become to a very considerable degree a fixed cost. This is in an economy with very high levels of capital investment to meet rapidly increasing demand, and with most of that investment financed by bank borrowings which carry fixed charges. There is, then, characteristically a rather high level of fixed costs for Japanese companies to which is added the labor component. It is of course true that labor is not entirely a variable cost of Western companies; not all of the labor force can be discharged on brief notice. The relative difference is very great however.

The results are twofold. First, there is a clear incentive, when faced with reduced demand, or lower demand than anticipated, to operate facilities at capacity so long as a price can be obtained that is greater than variable costs. This can be a low price indeed. The Western tendency is more likely to be a cutback in output since a more considerable proportion of costs can be reduced.[1] Second, the effects of a demand level that is lower than anticipated can result in enormous swings in profitability and severe difficulties for the less efficient producers in an industry. In this way, as well as in terms of the long-run effects of the employment system on costs, the Japanese economy can be a punishing environment indeed for the inefficient producer.

The Problem of Mergers

A very considerable disadvantage to the economy of the employment system is its impact on the possibility of effective merger of companies, or the acquisition of one company by another. It is exceedingly difficult, in fact nearly impossible,

---

[1]This analysis is more fully developed by James C. Abegglen and William V. Rapp, "Japanese Managerial Behavior and Excessive Competition," *The Developing Economies*, Vol. VIII, Number 4, pp. 427–444 (December 1970).

to combine two large and reasonably healthy Japanese companies. Even when there has been a long history of previous combination, as with Yawata and Fuji Steel or the three Mitsubishi companies that now comprise Mitsubishi Heavy Industries, combination once again was hard to bring about.

The principal reasons have to do with personnel. There is the obvious difficulty of settling on titles and ranks. There is the further difficulty of agreeing on personnel practices. Putting two unions together is a terrible task. More important, the employment system makes it virtually impossible in any reasonable period of time to realize the potential cost benefits of these mergers. Only attrition, a slow process in any event, allows the kind of work force reduction that is likely to be the principal potential advantage of merger.

The result is that while Japan is happily free of the preoccupation regarding sheer company size that handicaps the U.S. economy in particular, it is difficult to take full advantage of the potential for combination. Japan's fragmented paper and pulp industry is an example of the problem. Even though the present Oji, Jujo and Honshu paper companies were prewar a single entity, and merger was seriously discussed a few years ago, the issues of personnel frustrated the merger effort to the competitive disadvantage of Japan's industry.

In consequence, rather than full merger even when companies are in difficulties that merger alone will alleviate, a pattern has developed whereby the failing company survives as a legal corporate entity and continues production but its product line, facilities and sales functions are rationalized with that of a successful firm. This allows for many of the scale and other benefits of combination without requiring formal merger. This pattern has been particularly marked in the auto and agricultural machinery industries and more recently in consumer electronics.

Problems of International Management

There is reason to think that the special nature of Japanese employment practices may pose problems for Japanese management as it undertakes directly-owned operations outside Japan. Certainly the experience of negotiations with Japanese trade unions provides little by way of training for dealing with the unions of Britain and the United States. Then, too, it may well be even more difficult to integrate foreign nationals into executive positions in Japanese companies than has been the case with U.S. firms that are heavily invested abroad.

Something of the nature and extent of these problems might be gained from the experience of foreign firms in the Japanese economy. The problem of recruiting and retaining suitable personnel is almost certainly the greatest difficulty foreign investors have encountered in their Japan operations. The wholly-owned foreign firm is at an immense handicap in obtaining first class personnel; IBM is one of the very few firms which seems to have successfully dealt with this problem and which is seen as a highly desirable employer by university graduates. Foreign bank operations and airline offices have been plagued by union problems. Indeed, personnel considerations are not far behind government restrictions in comprising a barrier to direct foreign investment in Japan.

Just as lack of established position and experience in handling personnel issues are problems for the foreign operation in Japan, so they may become problems as Japanese companies undertake direct investment abroad. The issue is one of the future, but a not-distant future.

Changes in Japan's Employment System

Is the system of employment practices that has developed in Japan changing? The answer seems to be that it is not changing in any basic or extensive way. The suggestion that change is taking place in this pattern is a recurring one. Often examples are given of individual changes in employment that are taken as evidence that the system is undergoing modification. These seem still to be what they have proved to be in the past, individual cases that offer little by way of evidence of broader shifts.

Certainly some change has occurred at the margins of the system. There is now a group of Western business school educated younger Japanese who are detached from the system and will contemplate changing employers. There is a larger group in the labor force who, in one way or another, often through employment by the American occupation forces immediately after World War II, are outside the system and are prone to change jobs often. These tend to make foreign businessmen in Japan believe that more change is occurring in the total system than is in fact the case.

There are changes going on at the margins of compensation policy. Merit, productivity and rank considerations have some influence on compensation. It is still a modest influence. Retirement practices are under some pressure, with efforts to introduce flexibility into the "retirement at age 55" rule. The first efforts at introduction of pension programs are underway. However, 55 remains the general retirement age, and pensions remain rare and very limited in size.

Clearly any set of practices in an economy changing as rapidly as Japan's must come under some degree of stress and undergo some modification. It is hardly remarkable that employment practices would be discussed, reexamined, worried over, and to some degree altered. Any reasonable view of the past two decades however must conclude that continuity is the predominant fact, and that substantial change, while often heralded, is yet to occur.

Nor is this surprising. The system of employment in Japan

is a highly efficient one, and one that is congruent with the main values and behavior patterns of Japanese society. It is in many ways a more human, less brutal system of employment than the West has developed. It certainly is characterized by less conflict. Both its economic effectiveness and its social value work to maintain the system.

Will the system change? Of course. As the society changes, and it is changing, under the impact of affluence, increased leisure, a much altered pattern of family life and a greatly increased interaction with other nations, so patterns of relations in the workplace will change. Changes in the employment system will arise from these more basic social changes, and will reflect in the future as to date the characteristics of the broader society.

Part II

THE
JAPANESE FACTORY,
1956

Industrialization is a product of Western culture, and was long limited to those nations whose social patterns and historical experience was in or derived from Western Europe. Japan is the first nation outside this pattern, the first country to industrialize successfully whose social organization and cultural history are quite different and separate from the West. It would appear to follow, then, that industrial organization in Japan must take a pattern different from the West in order that industrialization may take place in this very different society. And this is in fact the case; the organization of labor resources in the Japanese workplace differs significantly from the Western pattern, is generally consistent with broader social patterns unique to Japanese society, and helps explain Japan's economic performance.

1.

INDUSTRY IN ASIA:
THE CASE OF JAPAN

THE PRESENT concern about the entire problem of industrialization has been compelled by the massive confrontation of the world's two great power centers. This confrontation is now taking place in the economic and industrial spheres, and the lives of most of the people of the world will be shaped irrevocably by the choice made in economic development between these power centers or some alternative approach to industrialization.

The choices of the route to industrialization cannot appear attractive to uncommitted nations. There is the Western alternative, industrialization arising out of a matrix including colonial exploitation, religious justification, and private, if not free, enterprise, a rapid but not meteoric change extending over some two centuries, wasteful of both time and resources. The Soviet alternative, posed again by China, affords the maximum of rapidity, the minimum use of external resources in capital, equipment, and personnel, and a surety of success from the very price paid—the terrible destructiveness of private and personal choice, initiative and freedom.

To the Asian or African these must seem dubious alternatives indeed. In terms of the preservation of the values and ideals precious in his present "underdeveloped" world, the outcomes might well appear mutually distasteful. From the one direction there is a welter of commercialism, restlessness, con-

fusion, and competition; from the other a monolithic and brutal
orderliness—monochromatic, intemperate, and unrelaxing.
Both alternatives threaten the erosion or destruction of his re-
ligion, his family system, and the tastes, habits, and even dress
and speech produced over millennia. These areas are not
"underdeveloped." They have developed fully but in a direction different from that which events now compel. There is
little choice about the fact of change. The change will come and
is now in process; the mode and the direction of change pose
these rude alternatives.

It is at this point that Japan becomes of special interest.
Japan is the single third party present now on the scene, a non-
Western nation that might properly be described as industrial,
which for all its industry remains clearly and consistently Asian.
Japan has changed greatly in the century since it reentered the
world; it has incorporated new ideas, adapted its older institutions, and accommodated to alien and often distasteful modes.
Still it remains true that Japan cannot be described in the terms
used in describing a nation of the West. It is not simply a re-
location of the arts, family system, social relations, or habits of
thought that have come to be associated with industrialization
throughout Europe and America. In some manner this enormous change in economic activity has been taken into an on
going culture and made into what might prove to be still
another approach.

The unique experience of Japan as a non–Western industrialized nation poses an exceptional opportunity for those interested in the process of industrialization in other Asian nations.
There is raised first of all a question, outside the scope of this
report, as to how this process took place, a historical question
concerning the causes and sources of this change. Another
question, and the central question of this study, is the outcome
of the process of industrialization in Japan. There is a marked
tendency to view industrialization in terms of particular West-

ern experiences—the Protestant ethic as a source of motivation, a trend to impersonalization of social interaction, the development of a rational world view by Western man. The question presents itself, then, as to how Western technology, modern industrial technology, may be fitted into a non–Western context with a different social inheritance. What kinds of adjustments must take place to fit this technology and the local peoples into an effective industrial unit?

These statements do not say or imply that Japan will furnish a case study from which may be predicted the course of industrialization in Indonesia, Burma, and India. Whatever the temptation to speak generally of Asia, this kind of generalization cannot be made from one to another of such enormously diverse cultures and peoples. The experience of Japan does provide, however, one test of the limits of adaptation, a measure of the kinds of alternatives to the technology-human relations interaction seen in the West which can be useful in attempting to estimate the range of adaptations and adjustments possible or necessary in introducing a technology which is the product of one kind of culture into another culture.

Apart from the several scientific questions implicit in this issue, there are some immediate and practical problems involved. As the West in general, and the United States in particular, embarks on programs to aid the economic development of non–Western nations, our ambassadors and envoys are drawn in large numbers from the ranks of engineers and businessmen, groups whose experience is usually confined to a single nation. Such personnel are clearly necessary and appropriate for the job to be done. Unfortunately, it seems true that ethnocentrism is particularly strong in the area of technological and business procedures. Thus there is a tendency to assume that since, let us say, job evaluation is useful and effective in American industry, it will be similarly useful and effective, even essential, in the industrial plants of Indonesia. If time study is a prerequisite to the effective use of machines in a plant in Ohio, the thinking goes, it must also be introduced into the organization of a plant in Shikoku. Perhaps these techniques should be used, but these industrial methods assume a great deal about the setting and people and involve problems of which the consultant or advisor might well be totally unaware. Although these are bread-and-butter problems, they illustrate a more general trend of thought about larger issues of organization and management. Furthermore, these small issues themselves can, and on occasion do, become major factors in the success or failure of American attempts to aid industrialization in different cultures. The study of industrialization in Japan may make possible a closer examination of some of the limits of these procedures and of the adaptation in the Western production system that may be necessary.

This, then, is the broad context in which this study of Japanese industrial organizations should be viewed. To bring about more effectively the orderly and rapid economic development of other nations and to make this technology fit more effectively into the ongoing patterns of social relations in non-Western nations, there is an urgent need for a further understanding of the outcomes of the introduction of modern industrial technology into cultures markedly different from our own. From the study of the outcomes of the Japanese experience, the methods employed in the social organization of Japanese factories, and the problems posed at present in Japanese industry by the lack of fit between technology and social custom, an approach to economic development in Asia might better be conceived.

A further objective of the study reported here was to add to the understanding of modern Japan through the detailed examination of a limited problem. Leaving aside descriptions of Japan by self-exiled romantics and the results of war-fevered attention, a very considerable part of the studies of Japan move on a quite general level. Attention to Japan's history and art has been substantial; but in speaking of modern Japan there is a distressing frequency of sentences beginning, "The Japanese are . . .", which treat the nation and its people as a compact and homogeneous unit with little or no note of the diversity and complexity of this modern nation. Most general is the view of Japan as a nation of fishing villages and farming hamlets, isolated communities, and ancient festivals. Although these elements are present in modern Japan, to understand the nation they must be seen in focus with Japan's sprawling, ugly cities, jammed with people, interlaced by high-speed transportation, smoky and noisy, and filled with the clamor and tension of commerce and industry.

There is a need for particularistic studies, aimed at the more detailed examination of problem areas which will spell out the full scope of diversity and complexity, to provide a more balanced view of Japan. It is to this end that studies of the Japanese factory might contribute. Despite the importance of Japanese industry in world economic affairs and the constant interaction, both friendly and competitive, between Western and Japanese enterprises, such studies are few in number. The importance of the topic, no less than the paucity of specific information, encouraged this report on some aspects of Japanese factories.

The study of the social organization of Japanese industry is thus taken to derive its relevance, first, from the intrinsic interest and importance of Japanese industry in the understanding of Japan and, second, from the possible implications of the Japanese experience and outcomes in industrialization for economic development of other non–Western countries. It might be hoped that a further by-product of such studies would be a contribution to the understanding of our own industrial organizations. Although the experimental methods as commonly conceived cannot usually be applied to persons or cultures, it is possible to approximate an experimental comparison of two cultures which will cast light on the underlying social dynamics of both cultures. The ethnocentrism referred to earlier has no doubt interfered with effective understanding of our own industrialization. Comparison with a nation like Japan may well further understanding of the United States.

Within this general framework of goals this study had as its objective a more particular problem. The emphasis on economic development of nonindustrial societies has led to a considerable interest in the history of the Japanese transition to industrialization. Analyses of the process of industrialization and the causes of economic development in Japan proceed, generally, on the assumption that the outcome of industrialization in that country has been, in terms of social organization and interpersonal relations, largely identical with the outcomes of industrialization in the West.

For example, a recent discussion of the social basis for Japan's rapid industrialization described as the outcome of the process the appearance of "an entirely different sort of social relationship than had been common in either China or Japan," and continues, "In the sphere of relationships industrialization carried with it an emphasis hitherto unequaled in social history on what the sociologists speak of as highly rational, highly universalistic, and highly functionally specific relationships."[1] The analysis of industrialization in Japan seems generally to proceed on the assumption that there occurred a transition from an earlier system of interpersonal relationships to this pattern of interpersonal relationships, a transition to the kind of interactions between people observed to be characteristic of Western societies under conditions of industrialization.

---

[1]Marion J. Levy, Jr., "Contrasting Factors in the Modernization of China and Japan," in *Economic Growth: Brazil, India, Japan*, Simon Kuznets, Wilbert E. Moore, and Joseph J. Spengler, eds. (Durham: Duke University Press, 1955).

The assumption that the results of industrialization in Japan have paralleled and been similar to those witnessed in the West not only underlies much of the academic analysis of the nature of the Japanese experience in the transition to an industrial economy but also is implicit in much of the effort to increase productivity in the Japanese factory. Owing in part to this assumption, methods and machines useful in British and American production are introduced into the Japanese factory with little attention to their appropriateness for what may be a markedly different organizational context. The assumption of similarity in organizational systems and in relationships in industry is in error. As a consequence, some of the analyses of the causes of Japan's industrialization as well as much of the effort to increase Japanese production do not achieve their purpose.

The close relationship between the organization of the total society and the organization of its industry has been demonstrated by considerable research in recent decades.[1] Given this evidence, it might be argued that, as a result of the differences between Japan and the West in preindustrial and present social organization, the present organization of the factory would differ in systematic ways in the two types of societies. Thus the social outcomes of technological change would not fit the pattern anticipated from a projection of the Western outcomes onto Japanese society. Again, the view that the Meiji Restoration and surrounding events constituted a basic and thoroughgoing revolution in Japanese society has been modified by indications that the changes in Japan after the 1860's grew out of earlier trends, impulses, and events and that the element of social discontinuity has been overstated in describing these eventful

---

[1]Important early contributions to this now substantial literature include Elton Mayo, *The Human Problems of an Industrial Civilization* (New York: The Macmillan Company, 1933), and F. J. Roethlisberger and W. J. Dickson, *Management and the Worker* (Cambridge: Harvard University Press, 1939), as well as the work of W. Lloyd Warner, William A. Whyte, and others.

decades.[1] Thus it might be argued that, whatever form industrial organization has taken in Japan, as an outgrowth of earlier
forms of social organization, it would be systematically different
from the Western model.

This report was shaped by the fact that the question of the
degree of resemblance between industrial organization in the
West and in Japan has been but little explored. This statement
is especially true of the large business firm, on which no literature is now available in English for the interested observer;
small firms as well have been reported on but little.[2] Indeed,
with the lack of a tradition of and interest in empirical field
studies in Japanese social science, especially in the fields of
sociology and psychology, there is little relevant information
available in Japanese literature.[3] The research conducted for
this report was therefore exploratory in nature. For this reason
and because the area of study was a broad and complex one and

---

[1]See, especially, George B. Sansom, *The Western World and Japan: A Study
in the Interaction of European and Asiatic Cultures* (New York: Alfred A. Knopf,
1950), and Donald Keene, *The Japanese Discovery of Europe: Honda Toshiaki
and Other Discoverers, 1720–1798* (London: Routledge and Kegan Paul, Ltd.,
1952).

[2]Two papers which discuss the small factory in Japan are John Pelzel,
"The Small Industrialist in Japan," *Explorations in Entrepreneurial History*,
Vol. 7 (December 1954), and Lawrence Olson, "A Japanese Small Industry:
A letter from Kyoto," *Explorations in Entrepreneurial History*, Vol. 8 (April
1956).

[3]Commenting on this field, a leading Japanese sociologist remarked, "Research on industrial relations and union problems in our country has been
deficient in close analyses of human relations in organizations and in unions.
No small part [of such studies] are very general discussions...critical 'theories'
which dispense with detailed investigation, various legal discussions, arguments for institutional reform, and ideological controversies. Summing up,
these comments will indicate the low level of social science in this country.
For these reasons we feel very strongly the necessity of promoting in this
country detailed, close researches on issues in human relations." Odaka
Kunio, *Sangyo ni okeru Ningen Kankei no Kagaku* (Science of Human Relations
in Industry) (Tokyo: Yuhikaku Kabushiki Kaisha, 1953), p. 178.

an intimate grasp of the setting, Japan, is not readily achieved by the external observer, this report is in no way complete or final. Rather, it is an attempt, on the basis of limited observation, to set out the broad outlines of the organization of the Japanese factory.

It will be the burden of this report to show that, whatever their similarities in technology and external appearance, the American and Japanese factory organizations differ in important ways. Examining in turn the nature of the basic relationship between employee and firm, the recruitment of personnel by the company, and the systems of rewards employed in the factory, consistent differences will be seen, differences which have immediate and important effects on the kind of technology and management methods that can be used in the organization. Further, it will be seen that within the organization the extent and nature of the involvement of the firm in the life of the worker are based on different assumptions as to the nature of the work relationship.

In short, in the critical areas of interpersonal relations and group interaction, in the definition of the nature of the relationship between worker and company, and in the way in which skills and energies are mobilized and directed in the group, the Japanese factory is a variant of industrialization from the American factory. These variations may be seen as deriving essentially from the differences between the broader social systems of the United States and Japan. An understanding of these variations is essential to an understanding of Japanese industry. From the Japanese experience, too, relevant clues may be gained as to the kinds of problems that may be encountered with the introduction of industrial technology into other non–Western nations.

2.

THE CRITICAL DIFFERENCE:
A LIFETIME COMMITMENT

WHEN COMPARING the social organization of the factory in Japan and the United States one difference is immediately noted and continues to dominate and represent much of the total difference between the two systems. At whatever level of organization in the Japanese factory, the worker commits himself on entrance to the company for the rest of his working career. The company will not discharge him even temporarily except in the most extreme circumstances. He will not quit the company for industrial employment elsewhere. He is a member of the company in a way resembling that in which persons are members of families, fraternal organizations, and other intimate and personal groups in the United States.

This rule of a lifetime commitment is truly proved by its rare exceptions, and the permanent relationship between employee and firm imposes obligations and responsibilities on both the factory and the worker of a different order than that on which personnel practices and worker-company relationships in the United States are built. The difference between the two systems is not, of course, absolute, but one of degree. Reluctance on the part of the worker to quit and on the part of the firm to fire him are constant factors in the American relationship; the Japanese firm will discharge employees, and employees do occasionally quit. The magnitude of the difference is very great, however, and its consequences and implications will be seen repeatedly throughout this description of the large Japanese factory.

To illustrate the Japanese practice the labor exit rates of two large firms for several years will be examined. The first is an electrical equipment manufacturing firm in the Osaka area. The company employs some 4,350 persons, of whom five or six are fired each year, or about one per thousand. These discharges are for reason of extreme behavior—e.g., a man who had not been in the plant for some weeks, following a series of similar absentee periods, or a worker accused of habitual and substantial thievery of company property—that is, the breach of conduct is so considerable as to allow no alternative to discharge.

As to labor exits for reasons other than discharge, the annual rate for the five-year period 1949–1953 was 83 out of 3,337 men and 109 of a total of 1,014 women, or a labor departure rate of between 2 and 1 percent for men and about 10 percent for women. Of the men, about two-fifths had reached retirement age; the remainder left the company for reasons of health or, more often, to return to the family farm after the death of a father or brother. (Since 1953 the exit rate for male employees in this firm has actually dropped and in 1956 was at the rate of 1.7 percent.) Among the women, since very few continue in the company's employ until their retirement age of 50 years, marriage, not age, accounted for almost all of the exits. Although there is no absolute sanction against married women working, in this company, as in all others, both company pressure and social custom almost demand that a married woman leave the job market.

It must be noted here that temporary layoffs because of lack of work do not take place in this or any other firm encountered in the course of this study. The company has full responsibility for the continued salary of all its employees for the duration of their employment, which is usually the full term of the working career. It is no wonder then that workers are often termed "permanent" or "eternal" employees.[1]

This firm is in no way exceptional in the exit rate of its employees. The highest annual rate of exit encountered in the large factories studied was in a textile plant in Shikoku, employing about 3,500 workers. Here the annual rate of exit for men over the five-year period 1951–1955 was 3.6 percent. This comparatively high percentage was caused by the plant's rural location, the rate of return to rural occupations being somewhat higher than usual. The exit rate for women was about 14 percent annually, again somewhat higher than in the urban plant.

These percentages include both management personnel and workers. An example of the exit rate of top management personnel taken alone is provided by the situation in a Tokyo firm. Top management was composed of 14 men, only 6 of whom had entered the firm immediately on completion of their schooling. At first sight this figure appeared to be a sharp departure from the general rule cited above, but closer examination proved it to be no exception. The firm was a member of one of the major prewar *zaibatsu* or cartel groups. Of the 8 men whose careers were seemingly spent in large part outside this company, 5 had come to the company from the *zaibatsu*

---

[1]The description of job relations given here is held to describe the general rule in the large factories of Japan. In a few types of industries, notably in construction and shipbuilding, worker recruitment and intraplant relations differ somewhat from those described in this report. Also, in the smaller and specialized shops of the large cities (e.g., in printing), movement of a worker from one job to another is more common and accepted. In the textile industry, where the proportion of female employees is high, data on the rate of exit of female workers provides an apparent exception to the above rules. Since women are expected and encouraged to marry, even assisted in marriage, after five to seven years of employment and must leave the company at the time of marriage, the rate of employee exit is high, which does not, however, alter the nature of the commitment of worker and company through the employment period.

bank and one from the trading company.[1] In short, both top management and workers stand in the same lifetime relationship to the company. The exceptions in no way negate the rule.

Viewing the overall social organization of the Japanese factory, it is clear that the lasting commitment of employee and employer, by which the employer will not discharge or lay off the worker and the worker will not leave the company's employ, is the result of and a striking example of a major difference between Western and Japanese job relationships. The Western relationship is more nearly "contractual." Both parties to the contract note that under certain conditions not necessarily related to the performance of his job the worker will be free to leave the company's employ and the company will be free to ask him to leave. He may be offered by another company a higher position, more pay or leisure, more opportunity for advancement, or a better location. He may, within specified rules, terminate the relationship and, more important, if he does so no particular stigma attaches to his leaving. On the contrary, he may well be seen as a more intelligent, more ambitious, more able person for having found a better position. In the same manner, the company, while more limited in its discretion, may for reasons usually having to do with its financial position terminate the relationship.

A rather high rate of movement from job to job and company to company characterizes both American workers and executive personnel. Generally, a high rate of mobility is considered desirable in American business. Such terms as "the free play of the labor market" and "cross-fertilization of man-

---

[1]The remaining two apparent exceptions were of special interest in terms of the interrelations of business and politics in Japan. One of these men did not join the firm until he was 62 years of age; he had been a judge in an important court in the Japanese judicial system. The other, who entered the company at the age of 61, was and is a member of the Diet's majority party. He was also the only nonuniversity graduate among the top management group.

agement" convey the belief that the limited job commitment and limited worker-firm relationship are usually advantageous so long as the rate of movement does not interfere with continued presence of trained personnel.

Although the system of job relationships employed in Japan might be supported by the argument that it ensures the continued use of company-trained personnel, the rationale presented by Japanese management ordinarily emphasizes other points. Its policy toward dismissals and layoffs is usually explained in terms of larger national issues and problems. The most frequent justification offered is that Japan is a poor country and an overpopulated one, a country where jobs are scarce and employment difficult. Laid-off or dismissed workers will simply starve, the argument goes, because they will be able to find no other work. For the employees' sakes, therefore, the company must ensure continued salaries at all times. This approach to employment is also justified in terms of the national welfare. Since jobs are scarce and the population large, it is the duty of management to maximize the number of positions in the plant and refrain from reducing the work force. In the interest of the national economy management has a duty to employ as many people as possible at all times.

These arguments on the part of Japanese management to justify its personnel policy are worth fairly close attention. They are revealing both of management thinking in Japan and of the broader underlying interpersonal relations in the factory. First of all, Japanese management at all levels is prone to think in large national terms and is quite conscious of the interaction between business policy and national welfare. This concern for the national well-being is no doubt a consequence both of the historical intimacy of government and business in Japan and of the high consciousness of the impact of business policy on national welfare in a nation so dependent on import-export exchange for its survival.

The argument that Japan is a poor country has become a national cliché. It is applied to virtually all inconveniences and discomforts in Japan, with, on occasion, no apparent connection between the problem and the announced poverty. In relation to employment practices, it might well be argued that the national economy would be aided by an increased efficiency in factory output resulting from increased labor mobility and a responsiveness of the work force to the workings of supply-demand factors. The argument justifying permanent employment in terms of national well-being might be seen most accurately as a rationalization of a system rather than as an explanation of a real cause of the system of job relations.

In addition to the argument concerning national economic welfare, another aspect of the explanation by Japanese management of the factory-worker relationship should be noted. Japanese management argues that laid-off or discharged workers will face financial disaster and the company therefore must not lay off and may fire workers only in cases of extreme provocation. It is true that a worker of whatever competence is hard put to find new employment if it is known (and his age will indicate) that he has been fired or laid off from a job. This becomes a circular problem, however. Since, under the present system. layoff means incompetence of the most drastic sort, it is not surprising that a layoff or discharge on a man's work record is taken automatically to mean that he is not suitable for further employment.[1] The system is in this way self-reinforcing. Again the argument is more a rationalization of the existing system than a convincing analysis of the reasons for the permanent employer-employee relationship.

---

[1] In this connection it is interesting to note the complaints of American businessmen in Japan that they are not able to hire first-rate Japanese college graduates. The threat of a limited work period and the subsequent difficulties in reestablishing themselves in the Japanese business world make the Western firms an insecure job avenue for these young men.

In a purely economic definition of employment terms, where the financial success of the factory is the overriding goal of management's policy, the national well-being and workers' welfare would be secondary considerations in much policy formation. Underlying the specific points made in support of the Japanese policy, and quite aside from the validity of these points, is the tacit recognition by management that the relationship between the company and the worker is not simply a function of the economic convenience of the two parties. The worker, whether laborer or manager, may not at his convenience leave the company for another position. He is bound, despite potential economic advantage, to remain in the company's employ. The company, for its part, must not dismiss the worker to serve its own financial ends. Loyalty to the group and an interchange of responsibilities—a system of shared obligation—take the place of the economic basis of employment of worker by the firm.

The area of mutual interchange of responsibility and obligation goes considerably beyond the regulations and practices governing employment and dismissal. Taking this one factor alone, however, wide-ranging and serious consequences of this permanent kind of job relationship may be mentioned.

In the Japanese factory at the present time it is commonly noted and readily admitted that there is almost always a surplus of labor over the number required to maintain the level of production. By American factory standards there is an astonishing proliferation of make-work jobs, jobs often of a menial sort—tea servers, sweepers, messengers, doorkeepers, and the like—which could be substantially and easily reduced in number, as well as a great deal of inefficient use of time and energy in productive jobs.

Using American standards it is not possible to compare directly the productivity of Japanese and American factories. For example, since the greater part of unit cost in American production is usually assumed to be labor costs, it is mandatory to maximize the use of machine processes in production. The reverse is true in Japan, where labor costs are such that the machine is the luxury and the laborer the lower-cost productive unit. However, the fact remains that even within the Japanese system of production the typical factory has a substantial surplus of workers, which is a direct result of the inability of management to lay off or dismiss workers.

There are further consequences of this labor immobility which affect seriously the economic well-being of the factory and the nation. They are felt in two particular aspects of the economy. The first is that of technological change. Clearly, where a surplus of laborers presently exists there is a much reduced incentive to introduce new methods of machinery into production. The result is to enhance a conservative attitude toward change which is already fairly strong in the thinking of factory management. However, it is not possible for management to totally resist technological change. Several factors make for an inexorable shift toward increasingly mechanized, labor-saving production methods and an exacerbation of the problem of labor surplus. One of these is, of course, the output of new products, products obtained by purchase of foreign patents or, less often, through local development. The new product is adopted along with the more mechanized productive system devised when the product was developed in, say, Germany or the United States. Thus, comparable output of this product with the one it replaces is ordinarily less demanding of labor.

Another and more important factor in technological change, which leads to an increasingly severe labor problem, is the pressure felt by Japanese management to use new methods and new machines. Japanese management looks now, as in the early development of Japanese industry, to foreign and, at present, chiefly American, sources for ideas and techniques. These vary from particular engineering methods to those of general management. Insofar as new technology is introduced, however, it has nearly always had the effect of exacerbating the already present problem of labor surplus in the factory. It should be noted that this is a different kind of problem from that caused by the introduction of automation, for example, in an American firm. In the United States the problem might become a community or national one of a total surplus of labor; in Japan the labor surplus would present a serious problem for the management of the particular factory which introduced the change.

The second category of difficulty created by the worker-firm relationship in Japan has to do with the impact of sudden economic change on the factory. Here an example might be taken from recent history. In the early days of the postwar American occupation of Japan, a considerable economic inflation took place. On the recommendation of a committee of American financial advisors the Japanese government undertook in 1949 a rather sudden and considerable change in policy. One result was a drop in economic activity, known to Japanese businessmen as the "Dodge depression" in commemoration of the head of the advisory group. The effects on many companies were little short of catastrophic. Apart from such firms as those in textiles, the products of which were in little demand during the war years, as a result of wartime expansion most large firms were committed to very large work forces. They had managed to carry these employees through the early postwar years, but the situation in 1949 became such that they simply could no longer do so. In a number of companies this depression became the occasion for a kind of drastic surgery unprecedented in company history, a surgery that came to be known as "rationalization." This step called for heroic measures, and their magnitude indicates the extreme difficulty management has in adapting to sudden shifts in economic tides.

In one company the work force, both management and labor, was reduced in eight months from 3,926 to 3,206 persons.

About 600 workers and 125 staff members were "voluntarily retired." Although the term sounds ironic in the Japanese context, it appears that these were in fact voluntary retirements. Workers were offered their normal full retirement allowance plus a special allowance, the total payment in most cases amounting to about ¥500,000. Noting that the average monthly wage payment in this plant in 1949 was about ¥10,000 it will be seen that the inducement to retire was substantial—and enormously costly to management. Those who retired were largely older persons nearing normal retirement, who took advantage of the special allowance, and women who used the sum as a substantial addition to their dowries. In all, 15 percent of the firm's laborers left, 9 percent of the men and 32 percent of the women; and 9 percent of the staff retired, 5 percent of the men and 21 percent of the women. These were all voluntary retirements, and the special high cost is a measure of the great difficulties involved in adjusting the size of the work force in a Japanese factory.

This drastic move brought with it, it might be noted, two problems for the future which are currently worrying management. By lowering the average age of the work force, recent retirements have been few in number and will suddenly become considerable in the not-too-distant future. More awkward, since it was difficult to induce staff personnel to retire, a number of companies now have a large surplus of staff and managerial personnel, with resulting depressing effects on promotion rate, morale, and job efficiency.

The "Dodge depression" and its effect on this one plant may serve to make the point that, whatever the advantages of a continuing obligation on the part of the worker and firm to remain in relationship, it is extremely difficult to achieve any measure of flexibility of work force within the Japanese system. The 1949 economic crisis did not affect all plants and firms to the same extent; this "rationalization" was by no means universal. However, all Japanese factories have a similar set of problems arising from the same causes, even those firms which have shown an increase in plant size or total business.

A minor example of the difficulties arising out of worker immobility in an expanding firm might be taken from the experience of a large metals-processing firm. This company has plants in several parts of Japan, and a rather new installation is located in south-central Honshu. To attempt to reduce somewhat the oversupply of labor in other plants, an effort was made to staff the newer plant, as its production increased, with workers from other plants. This transfer had taken place from one of the plants studied. Of the 40 men assigned and moved to the new location, 2 had committed suicide within two weeks. Although the firm did not yet have enough information to be sure of the causes, there was a generally held view that the suicides were the result of the men's inability both to deal with the fact of being transferred and to adjust to the new situation. Although an extreme case, this example suggests that the immobility of Japanese labor is not merely an economic problem.

Alternatives to the rigidity of the work force are offered by two aspects of present-day Japanese factory organization that can serve as buffers against the consequences of economic and technological change. The most direct practice is the utilization of "temporary" employees. The overall rule discussed until now applies to the category of employees referred to as "permanent" or "regular," including all staff employees and the great majority of laborers. However, most plants have a group of employees toward whom they do not have the same measure of responsibility, and who do not participate in the relationship previously described. The number of these employees varies with the work demands in the plant, the maximum observed being about 10 percent of the total laboring force. Legally these temporary employees can be laid off after two months' employment. They are usually hired through the government employment offices and frequently represent agricultural labor surplus (persons of farm background are generally considered desirable employees). Previous factory experience or training is not necessary for their employment and they perform lower-level tasks, often at the lowest possible salary. Clearly this system of supplementary labor recruitment cannot replace in any substantial degree the primary system, but it does provide some measure of adaptability and flexibility to the work force. It should be added that workers ordinarily do not move from the ranks of temporary to permanent employees in the same company.

Another aspect of the Japanese factory system that plays some part in the amelioration of the consequences of the worker-firm relationship is the considerable number of affiliated and subordinate companies attached to a large factory. Subcontracting, sometimes within the plant of the parent company, often takes place. To the extent that increases in output might be met through subcontracting rather than through an attempted increase in productivity of the parent firm, the problem of increasing the labor force to meet increased business would be displaced to the smaller company. In general, however, subcontracting is confined to peripheral processes and to particular items. Further, it is no less difficult for the small firm to lay off or fire than for the large firm; indeed, in many ways it is more difficult. The union may play some part in maintaining the no-layoff rule and in ensuring its rigid adherence in the large firm, whereas the small plant will probably not be unionized. The personal relationship between employer and employee is strong in the small plant, however, and the rule of custom in the neighborhood or village in which the small plant is located is so effective that it is impossible, short of real bankruptcy, for most small factory owners to reduce their work force.

One further alternative for admitting some flexibility into the work force was reported, although it had not been resorted to for many years in any of the factories observed. In the event of a lack of work in the plants so complete as to preclude retaining the labor force, management has been able in the past to send workers home for a time. During this no-work period, the persons "laid off" continue to be employees of the company and are paid a salary of 60 percent of their usual income. This pay, despite no work performed, continues until the workers are recalled or the company dissolves as an organization. This device was resorted to during the depression of the 1930's and is not a factor in plant operations except in such an emergency period.

Since the immobility of the Japanese work force both within and between factories has so considerable an effect on the present functioning and future prospects of Japanese industry, and since it offers a clear contrast to the American practice, the problem has been examined here first and in some detail. The full meaning of this kind of worker-firm relationship, however, can be shown only in the wider context of the social organization of the Japanese factory. This kind of commitment between employee and employer is closely interrelated with the system of recruitment, the system of motivation and reward, and, indeed, is a basic part of the entire Japanese factory organization. Although it is possible to discuss the single aspect of the immobility of Japanese in isolation from the whole fabric of worker-firm relations, it does not function in such isolation, and to change this one element would affect profoundly the entire system. Before concluding that this is a disadvantageous employment system it is first necessary to look at other elements of the factory organization to gauge the effects of a possible change in this one factor.

3.

THE RECRUITMENT
OF PERSONNEL

A SYSTEM of organization in which membership is semipermanent may be expected to attach considerable importance to the recruitment and selection of its personnel. Where the job relationship is a more limited one, contractual and subject to termination, errors in selection need not weigh heavily in the successful operation of the organization. Where the employer-employee relationship is virtually irreversible and the commitment is for the career of both parties, errors in selection of organization personnel can seldom be rectified and demand a considerable price in organizational efficiency.

The Japanese factory presents a rather contradictory picture in terms of procedures for the recruitment and selection of personnel. There is an elaborate selection system in effect in the larger firms. At the same time, the basis for the selection of personnel and the avenues of recruitment are very different from those in the United States. The general difference lies in a greater dependence in selection in Japan on certain recruiting and selecting processes inherent in the broader social system—e.g., the relationship between student and teacher in the universities—and on qualities of character and background not directly related to the work position. Less attention is given to those qualities of the individual and methods of selection—e.g., aptitude and personality tests—which function in isolation from the social system and are evaluated in terms of potential performance on a specific job.

The selection of personnel in a Japanese factory is related more closely to education than to any other consideration. Both the categories of employees selected and the methods used in contacting and screening future employees depend very much on the way in which the Japanese schools are organized and on the reputations and personnel of the schools.

The Japanese educational system at the present time follows the 6–3–3–4 year pattern in common use in the United States. Introduced by the occupation authorities following the Second World War, the system is relatively new in Japan, and the people by no means unanimously support this system. Indeed, it appears likely that it will be modified in the future. However that may be, the present scheduling of education consists of six years of primary school, three of middle school, three of higher school, and four of college or university work.

The prewar system does not readily lend itself to a comparison with this American-style scheduling, since it was based on a European model. There were available specialized middle and higher schools providing occupational training in agriculture and industry for students who did not continue to a higher educational level. It is important to note, too, that graduation from the higher school of prewar Japan carried with it a level of accomplishment more nearly equivalent to graduation from an American junior college. Many problems, some of which will be apparent from the following discussion of factory recruitment, were created for Japan by the arbitary and shortsighted imposition of a sharply different system of educational scheduling. However, since the newer system is that on which present recruitment methods are based, it will be largely in terms of this division of education that current recruitment pratices will be described.

To provide a general indication of the nature of the relation between education and recruitment that exists in the Japanese factory, the figures in Exhibit I present the position in the organizational scheme and the education of all managers and supervisors and a 10 percent sample of wage and salary workers in a large manufacturing plant.

Exhibit I

POSITION IN THE FACTORY AND
EDUCATIONAL BACKGROUND

	Educational Background		
Factory Position	Primary and Middle School (%)	Higher School (%)	College or University (%)
Wage worker, female	100	0	0
Wage worker, male	100	0	0
Salary worker, female	11	89	0
Salary worker, male	16	73	11
Second-level supervisors	1	46	53
First-level supervisors	0	16	84
Top management	0	10	90

It will be noted that all wage workers are persons who have received no more education than that required by law. No persons who have received more than the minimal education are in the wage-worker group. Only about 15 percent of the salary workers, male and female, are less than high school graduates; and these, it should be added, are older persons, graduates of the former middle school. No female university graduates are employed in this particular plant. Three-fourths of the male salary workers are high school graduates, and the great majority of supervisors are college graduates. The sole member of top management not graduated from college was a graduate of the old-system higher school. The sharpness of differences by education between ranks is partially obscured in Exhibit I by combining the old and new systems. For example, the importance of college for selection into the supervisory and management level is concealed by the presence of graduates of the old-system higher school, actually equivalent to some college, in the higher school category.

Exhibit ı serves to provide a general picture of the intraplant situation. Three groups of workers may be broadly identified in the terms on which their selection is based. First of all there are the *koin* (literally, "persons who work"), the factory's wage workers, who have had a minimum of education. There is another broad group, *shokuin* ("persons in charge"), paid a salary and holding clerical and supervisory positions. In this *shokuin* group those persons who are high school graduates and occupy lower-level positions are distinguished from those who are college graduates occupying higher positions and eligible for the topmost rank.

In contrast to the American practice it must be emphasized that recruitment directly from schools into the company is to all intents and purposes the *only* way in which men enter the firm. When young Japanese businessmen are asked what they would do if offered a better position at more pay in another firm the general reaction is blank silence, a result of the fact that such an eventuality is so improbable—both the offer of another position and the possibility of accepting were it offered —that there is no response. The reaction from the more imaginative or speculative young man is amusement and interest in the possibility, followed by a flat and emphatic explanation that this is not going to happen and has not happened. This is, of course, another example of the immobility of personnel that heightens the importance of the educational system in the recruitment process.

To indicate the general methods of recruitment and their implications, the procedures actually followed in a representative company will be described. Typical of most firms, the hiring of clerical and future supervisory personnel in this particular large company is handled not by the local plant, as the laborers, but by the main office of the company; and, as with many other firms, the parent office is located in Tokyo, some distance from any of the firm's factories. The personnel department is divided so as to provide an entirely separate staff for the two broad groups of employees, *koin* and *shokuin*. The selection of university graduates expecially is watched most closely by top management and, in a sense, by the nation, for October, the examination month for the companies, is a critical time for many families throughout the nation.

Since the school year extends from spring to spring, rather than from fall to spring as in the United States, the process of selecting the young men who will someday manage the plant and company ordinarily begins in early fall from among those university students who will graduate in the spring. The procedures within each company are well defined. Most companies have a definite policy of not accepting applications directly from the individual job hunter. This firm considers about 40 college students yearly as candidates for employment. The company makes known to selected universities the number and type of openings available in the firm, and it is the prerogative of the university faculty to recommend individuals for examination by the company. In this firm's practice, only five of Japan's several hundred colleges and universities are considered. These five are Tokyo, Kyoto, and Hitotsubashi universities, state-supported, and Keio and Waseda universities, two leading private institutions. (It is important to note that four of these five universities are located in Tokyo.) Selection of men for general management training and advancement to management positions is made generally from the two curricula of economics and law. Most large Japanese universities do not have a direct equivalent of the American commercial or business curriculum.

Another part of the 40 applicants accepted are drawn from

the technical curricula of engineering, chemistry, and physics. In actual fact there is some difference in the selection procedure for these more technically trained college graduates. The company feels that in these curricula the professors come to know the competence and capacity of their students better than in the larger classes of the liberal arts curricula. As a result, a lesser number of candidates is selected, and the recommendation of the professor is nearly always sufficient for hiring. With these technically trained men the important factor in selection is not merely the university attended but the professor under whom the student has studied. The company looks for its electrical engineers from among the students of one professor at one university, and for its chemists among the students of a certain professor at another university. It is the prerogative and responsibility of these leading professors to allocate their students among the several large companies.

Final selection from among these 40 applicants accepted for further testing comes in October, and a quite elaborate battery of tests is employed, including a thorough physical examination. The large Japanese factory, including this one and all others observed, employs no one suffering any kind of physical disability. A family and personal history is also obtained. The core of the testing situation, however, is a series of intellectual examinations. To illustrate these a few of the questions employed are as follows:

A. Write an essay on freedom and regulation in economic life.
B. Discuss three of the following.
   1. Technological unemployment
   2. Liquid assets
   3. Variable capital and constant capital
   4. Proxy and mandate
   5. Conversion of public debt

C. Translate into Japanese the underlined sentences:
[In English] Human beings differ profoundly in regard
to the tendency to regard their lives as a whole. To some
men it is natural to do so, and essential to happiness to
be able to do so with some satisfaction. To others life is
a series of detached incidents without directed movement and without unity. I think the former sort are
more likely to achieve happiness than the latter since
they will gradually build up those circumstances from
which they can derive satisfaction and self-respect,
whereas the others will be blown about by the wind of
circumstance now this way, now that, without ever ar-
riving at any haven. The habit of viewing life as a whole
is an essential part both of wisdom and of true mora-
lity, and is one of the things which ought to be encouraged in education.

Questions A and B are of the type asked graduates of the law
and economics curricula; and for them are substituted more
technical questions on their specialities for would-be engineers
and research men. On the whole, however, these examples will
serve to illustrate the type and level of the company-given employment tests.

There can be no question of the severity of the screening
based on these tests and, inasmuch as the testing is coupled
with interviews, usually with selected members of the top management group, which also weigh heavily in the final selection,
there can be little doubt that the 10 or 12 men finally hired from
among these 40 candidates are indeed able. The question of
whether they are, on the basis of the results of their tests, appropriate candidates for top management positions was not
raised by management in the course of discussions of selection
procedures. The connection between competence on this kind
of test and managerial skill is certainly not a necessary one.

The example cited from this firm brings out the overall approach to the selection of college graduates. These men are taken from a sharply limited number of universities. Their very chance to apply for a job is dependent on their relations with their university professors. While in some companies more use is made of interviews, where the candidates are intensively examined by a group of ten or more members of top management, whether the interviews or tests are the prime instrument of selection, emphasis is placed on knowledge of a quite specialized sort. The examinations are designed to eliminate rather than measure, to reduce the numbers of candidates rather than probe out adequate candidates from a large group.

Looking now at the selection of high school graduates, the same company will be used to continue the illustration of Japanese recruitment and selection procedures. High school candidates in this firm are drawn from a wider geographical range of schools than are the college graduates. About 100 high schools are considered by the company to be of a level adequate to provide company employees. The company assumes that able students in the metropolitan areas will go on to college and that the candidates for employment from urban areas who have no college ambitions are seldom worth the company's attention. Thus these future clerical workers, male and female, are recruited largely from nonurban high schools. Less than one-third comes from the Kobe-Osaka area in which this company has most of its facilities; the rest come from a wide scattering of prefectures. Like the college graduates, these high school students are hired through the company's main offices and are assigned to the separate factories by the main office personnel department. There is an interesting difference in the general procedure, however. In connection with the hiring of college graduates the company makes known to certain universities its needs and wants in personnel; with high school graduates the principal of the school and the teachers approach the company asking that their student or students be considered as applicants for clerical positions. These men usually take some part of their summer vacation for this activity, and the placement of good students in good positions is seen as one of their responsibilities.

This firm examines 150 high school graduates annually, and from this number about 15 new employees are selected. The selection procedures are similar to those used for college students, again employing a battery of rather difficult academic examinations along with a physical examination and a more routine interview. Since the present high school system is comparatively new it is not possible to demonstrate statistically what appears to be a fact, that at present high school graduates are not considered eligible for higher managerial positions. This statement does not say that no exceptions to the college graduate rule may be found, but that they are very few in number, usually products of the older higher schools and well known throughout the company. It might be predicted that unless the older system of education is reinstituted, which is a real possibility, there will arise in time, and there is now in the process of development, a formally tripartite division of workers replacing the present dichotomy of *koin* and *shokuin*. Indeed, such a process seems well formulated in the National Railway Company; a few graduates of the top universities are hired annually for special positions with special income and training and assurance that they will someday become at least divisional superintendents.

Looking at the other group in the factory, the *koin*, and their entrance to the company, it is hard at present to generalize on admissions policies. At the present time few large Japanese factories are accepting new employees at this level. The problems of the work force size discussed above are such that general employment in the factory is virtually at a standstill, except for two groups. One is the apprentice group, still numerous in most plants, and the other is the temporary worker described above. Most managements consider themselves fortunate if they can restrict admissions at the worker level to a number no greater than the rate of retirement. Inasmuch as the "rationalization" effort sharply lowered the age level in many plants, retirements are few. Since workers do not quit unless they are leaving factory work entirely, there is at present little occasion to hire any large number of permanent employees.

It may, however, be assumed that the general attitude and methods governing the employment of apprentices are similar to those used in the employment of general factory laborers. A plant of the firm described here has as apprentices about 60 men and 100 women. The larger number of women is necessary to balance the higher turnover rate in female employees. The recruitment procedures for these future laborers are sharply different from those for future *shokuin*.

The intermediary in recruitment of laborers is the work stabilization office of the Japanese government which maintains employment offices throughout the country, and it is through these that members of the factory's personnel department contact potential employees. Only graduates of middle school are considered as candidates. Graduates of higher school are not wanted, although the personnel department believes that some 20 or 30 of the plant's 3,000 laborers have successfully disguised their higher school backgrounds and are now working as laborers. The policy of hiring minimally educated laborers is closely connected with the other major consideration of the company in employing new laborers—what has been phrased by the personnel department as a desire for persons with "stable natures." To find such persons, a considerable search is made for young men just out of middle school (aged 14 or 15) who are the sons of farmers, living in rural areas, and strongly desirous of finding urban, factory employment.

Some trouble is gone to at the present time to find these

"stable" young men and women. For example, about 10 percent of the current class of apprentices were recruited from Japan's southernmost major island, Kyushu, and from a particular agricultural area there. The company's experience with people from this area has been good; and, as a result, it sends representatives to the local employment office to recruit apprentices for employment in the distant cities. Candidates for laboring positions receive interviews and tests appropriate to their educational level but not less severe in length and intensity than those for higher positions. Included in this test battery is a brief paper-and-pencil intelligence and dexterity test.

Unlike the *shokuin*, the apprentice laborers are hired by the individual factories on the decision of the local personnel department. While the *shokuin* are transferred from factory to factory as needed and are assigned out of the main offices, the *koin* will remain in the plant for which they are hired for the remainder of their careers. Although it is possible for these apprentice laborers to be fired during the first several months of their employment as apprentices, they receive full status as permanent employees. They are under the supervision of long-service foremen, live together in the company dormitories, and in general are closely supervised and thoroughly integrated into the company from about the age of 15. As stated earlier, under present factory conditions not only this factory but also most other large plants are now hiring laborers only through this apprentice route, except for the temporary employees hired and fired as the work load demands.

It might be appropriate at this point to mention the recruitment of temporary employees, who are, of course, all laborers. As the apprentices, they are hired through the work stabilization offices of the government, and here, too, the company strongly prefers temporary employees from rural backgrounds. Experience is not necessary and these temporary workers are usually farm laborers, surplus agricultural labor, who ostensibly at least are to return to the farms when the company dismisses them, their term of employment averaging about five months. They are selected by members of the personnel department who first notify the government office in desired rural districts and then interview applicants in the local offices. In addition to the inevitable physical examination, the interview deals primarily with the man's personal background. He should have an average background, with a living standard "not too high and not too low;" he should not appear restless and should have a stable job history; and his education should not be too limited but must not exceed the present middle school level.

The preceding paragraphs have described the recruitment and selection methods in one Japanese factory, a firm quite representative of the general approach in the large Japanese manufacturing firms. The factors considered have been almost entirely formal ones, explicit and formalized requirements for admission into employment and thus into the permanent factory-worker relationship that distinguishes Japanese industry, but informal factors do play a part. Such matters, however, as family background, personality, and influential connections have their primary influence in terms of educational level achieved and play, insofar as could be determined, a distinctly secondary role in the actual employment process.

Still, nepotism and the like are factors in the employment system of the Japanese factory. In many cases the large Japanese company discourages and attempts to limit direct family relations among employees. For example, marriage among employees, particularly among *shokuin*, is disapproved of, and usually husband and wife may not both continue working for the company. Not only is the wife expected to retire but also the husband may find that the marriage has a markedly negative effect on his career progress. Although such marriages have increased slightly since the war, they are still few in number.

In a survey of one plant, about one out of four of the male workers in both factory and office and about one out of four of the female workers reported relatives in the employ of the company. This figure is probably somewhat higher than the average. The relationship was not often father-son or father-daughter but in the majority of cases was one of uncle-nephew or uncle-niece. Especially among female office workers—better educated and from higher status families—the presence of a family member in the work situation is seen by the family at least as most desirable. The bonds of obligation between brothers in the Japanese family help account for the high incidence of uncle-niece relations in the plant.

In addition to general disapproval of close relatives in the same work situation, two factors help depress the number of such cases. First, all new employees are subject to the same tests and interviews, and these eliminate a certain number of familial candidates. Second, it is held and operates as a negative factor that the son of a worker is unable or unwilling to advance himself educationally, and he is not considered a good employment risk.

The influence of family connections seems about the same for top management positions at the present time as for workers. In large firms direct family connections are not and have not been the rule, at least since the postwar changes in ownership and management of the large companies. In the two large firms in which this problem was investigated in some detail (and with some difficulty) about two out of ten of the top management group were directly related, as sons or nephews, to former or present top managers. These cases were those in which the father or uncle had previously been himself at the very top of the management hierarchy in the firm.

This proportion is most deceptive, however. Entrance to the very few universities from which it is possible to move into top management positions is largely confined to those students

whose educational and financial resources are well above average. That is, a considerable selection of "young men from good
backgrounds" takes place without the industrial firms themselves becoming directly involved in the process. By confining
management recruitment to a limited number of universities,
the importance of family background has already been magni-
fied. Family connections operate in still another way, and to
illustrate this the firm discussed previously might again be used.
It will be recalled that about 40 college graduates are considered
for employment annually. While the majority of these are con-
tacted on the recommendation of professors from the key universities, a certain number, estimated by the personnel department at 2 or 3 per year and probably more, are considered
candidates on the urging of important customers of the firm or
officials of this or related firms. These young men must be graduates of the designated universities and must undergo the
usual testing procedure, but the personnel officials admit that
the company is placed in an awkward position if these specially
recommended candidates fail their examinations.

In other words, the working of family influence is commonly
indirect in the large Japanese firm, but is very considerable
looking at the total recruitment process. Formally, most of the
large *zaibatsu* groupings have not yet reamalgamated, although the process of regrouping is well under way. Even without formal or official connections, however, relations between
these formerly interowned firms are intimate and friendly. As a
result, while the top official of a manufacturing firm might find
it awkward to provide a position for his son in his own company,
he is able to accommodate the sons of friends or relatives and to
arrange for a position of some importance for his own son or
nephew in a related firm. Thus the son of the former president
of a chemical company might now be an official in a trading
company, one which previously was directly connected with the
chemical company but which is now formally independent.

The full working out of all informal factors, including that of nepotism, in the recruitment and selection process, which would require the most detailed case studies of a large number of individuals, was beyond the compass of this study. Within these limits, however, the recruitment procedures, when taken together with that special relationship between worker and firm described in the preceding chapter, have important effects both on the internal functioning of the Japanese factory and for the nation as a whole. Seen most broadly, this system of recruitment does not fit well the present educational system in Japan and presents serious problems for the nation as a result of this lack of fit.

To review generally the differences in prewar and postwar educational scheduling, primary schools were attended by all under both systems. At primary school graduation a division took place in the older system, and the majority of youths, those with no chance to go on to higher school or college, attended a special middle school or a terminal higher primary school. These schools had the clear objective of providing the basic education for persons who would become farmers, laborers, and the like. Alternatively, youths whose families intended sending them to higher school or college went directly from primary to a general middle school.

Following middle school a division again took place in the older system between future college and noncollege students. About half of the middle school graduates attended a special higher school, usually to learn a trade; the half of the middle school students who planned university work attended a higher school designed to prepare them for college entrance.

It will be seen that the fit of the older system of education to the factory system of recruitment was a good one. Business firms received from the old-system higher primary schools individuals with a terminal lower level of education. At the present time, owing in part at least to the mixed objectives of mid-

dle school education, terminal for one group and preparatory
for another, many businessmen feel their workers are not well
prepared for factory work. In a nation where the average income is about $40 monthly, education for children beyond
the middle school level is a luxury few farming or laboring
families feel they can afford. Thus the pattern of high school
graduation common in America is not achieved in Japan except in a limited number of cases, and the utility of the American high school in holding potential workers off the job market
for a long period of time cannot be achieved in Japan.

More critical than the other tensions arising from the lack of
fit of the educational system to the work system is that which
occurs at the college level. In Japan for many years university
graduation conferred on the student the privilege of employment at a high level in business, the military, or the government. The student expected such employment, and at the same
time the pool of unemployed intellectuals that has plagued other
non–Western nations did not develop. This system required, of
course, a limited number of highly selected and trained university students. The increase in colleges resulting from the up-
grading of former higher schools to college status has increased
many times over the number of university and college students.
They are not employable at the higher white-collar level owing
to sheer numbers, and yet the attitude and expectations of both
students and employers remain as before: college graduates are
suitable for a certain kind of position only. Business firms formally, and government agencies informally, generally limit
their recruitment for potential management positions at the
present time to a small number of top-rated universities. The
result is both a great increase in the number of unemployed
college graduates and a furious competition for entrance to the
few highly ranked universities. However the notion may seem
to Americans, in the present Japanese context it is not bizarre
for a student to commit suicide after repeatedly failing to a-

chieve admission to a top university, despite the two or even three years spent after graduation from higher school in preparation for the entrance examinations.

This broad sketch will serve perhaps to indicate the nature of some of the issues raised for the nation by the critical role of education in Japanese industrial recruitment. Returning to the factory itself, two main effects may be noted at this point. The first is the effect of the recruitment system on the use of personnel in the factory and, second, the effects of the recruitment on relationships within the plant.

It has been seen that once employed a worker expects to remain indefinitely in the employ of the firm. He has been selected with some care, and once selected he is a permanent member of the firm until the end of his working career. In this system, once the worker has been selected, the company practically speaking foregoes the right to find the worker incompetent. He was not selected for a particular job or because he had acquired a particular set of skills useful in the operation of the plant. He was selected for qualities of background, personality, and general ability that may not in fact make him a competent employee. However, should the firm find him useless it cannot dismiss him but may only move him from job to job within the general category of his employment status until he is placed in a harmless and perhaps not useful position. Thus a young middle school graduate, once accepted into the worker-firm relationship, may finally become a sweeper or doorkeeper for reason of limited ability. A college graduate may be placed in a position as assistant to the least important section head and kept there for lack of ability. In any event, once admitted into employment, employees of Japanese firms will not be fired on grounds of lack of ability.

The consequences of this system in terms of efficient use of personnel need hardly be described. The proliferation of positions, the development of make-work jobs, and the loss of productivity from the retention of incompetent personnel are all clear and predictable. Conversely, the employee finding the company incompatible with his interests or ambitions or his work distasteful may not leave—except, of course, to enter a family business, return to the family farm, or open a small shop.

Another far-reaching effect of this system of recruitment within the company is its tendency to make for widely disparate groups of employees who are homogeneous within each group in experience and outlook but ill-equipped to communicate with each other. This system also has effects in terms of loss of potential leadership in the lower ranks by exclusion of *koin* from promotion to higher status, a point which will be examined further in terms of the internal career system of the factory. It may be noted now that the recruitment system establishes three groups of employees. Each group is made up of individuals from similar backgrounds and training. The groups are markedly dissimilar each from the other.

There is, first of all, a group of workers recruited from the middle schools of Japan. These workers are usually from rural backgrounds and from lower-status families. They are employed in a particular factory, are trained together for work in that factory, and enter a similar status in the factory as apprentices and unskilled laborers.

At the other extreme in the factory status system is that group of employees who are all graduates of universities and of the same or closely related universities. Whatever their place of origin, all of these employees have spent some years in a large urban center, almost always Tokyo. They enter the firm at the same level, and their identifications and loyalties are to the firm rather than to a particular factory. Their family backgrounds are at least middle class, and they are for the most part the sons of professional people, businessmen, or higher-status white-collar workers. In nearly all respects—family background, style of life, life chances, experience, and education—there are few points of contact or mutual attitudes, objectives, or experiences between this group and the first group of employees.

Somewhat intermediate to these two groups are those workers graduated from present-day higher schools, who are from a scattering of localities, often urban, sons and daughters of skilled workers and lower level white-collar workers, a more heterogeneous group sharing few of the experiences and characteristics of the extremes.

This outline of the recruitment and selection process in the Japanese factory is important to an understanding of the factory in two ways. In the first place, the system of recruitment is a part of and a reinforcement to the effects of the basic system of worker-firm relationships described earlier. Moreover, an understanding of the methods of recruitment and selection is essential to the understanding of the kinds of relationships within the firm and factory. The problems of pay and reward, career patterns and promotion opportunity, and interchange of obligations and responsibilities between employee and firm must be seen against the background of this approach to employee recruitment.

4.

REWARDS AND INCENTIVES
IN THE JAPANESE FACTORY

IN ANY SOCIETY or group the behaviors and modes of conduct most highly valued may be estimated by the degree to which those behaviors are rewarded by the group. The system of rewards may be examined to indicate both the kinds of behavior that the group hopes to elicit from its members and the kinds of behaviors which, through the system of reward, will be reinforced and perpetuated in the group. The study of the system of rewards and incentives employed in the large Japanese factory proved to be highly revealing of differences between Western and modern Japanese industry. It also served to demonstrate both the type and the magnitude of differences in the underlying attitudes and behaviors that differentiate modern industry in Japan from that in the United States.

In the following discussion, the pay system of one factory will be examined in detail to illustrate certain central tendencies observed in all the plants studied. Inasmuch as the system of monetary pay for work performed is only a part of the total system of rewards, the general pattern of extramonetary benefits, welfare activities, and worker incentive programs will be examined, again using specific programs and costs from particular plants. In addition, a typical retirement program will be outlined. On the basis of this data a general summary of the underlying features of the Japanese system will be undertaken and an effort will be made to compare the systems of rewards in Japan and the United States. Although there has been a good deal of discussion comparing wage levels in the two countries, most particularly with respect to textile production, these comparisons can be accurately made only when the entire wage program and reward system of the Japanese factory is examined.

The firm that will be used as an illustrative case study of the Japanese pay system is a metals-processing firm, employing some 3,400 persons, located in the Osaka-Kobe area. This firm is a relatively large one in Japan, a major producer in its field, and produces about half of its production for export. It is related to one of the large industrial combinations of prewar Japan. In short, it is an important and reputable company, and in both management policy and union history presents no special features obscuring the present overall discussion.

As in the firm previously described there are two groups of company employees, *shokuin* and *koin*; but the *koin* group is further divided in this firm into monthly and daily paid workers (that is, workers whose wages are computed on the basis of daily or monthly pay). Workers with one year's seniority are promoted from the daily to the monthly paid group. Temporary workers numbered only 56 at the time of the study. The average age of all employees was 35.6 years, with 10.4 years the average length of service (wartime interruptions accounting for the relatively low average length of service).

As in all large Japanese plants, the pay system here is complicated. The reference point in the system of calculation is a fixed amount which is termed base, or standard, pay. All factory laborers begin as daily paid *koin* in this plant. Their initial base pay is a function of age at the time of entrance, with about ¥54 paid to workers aged 14 years and about ¥94 paid those 22 years of age or more. The initial base pay of employees hired as *shokuin* is a function of education, with a monthly base pay of ¥3,950 for graduates of the old university system, ¥3,700 monthly for graduates of the new university system, and ¥2,500 monthly for new-system high school graduates. (At the time of this study [1956], the rate of exchange was ¥360 for one U.S. dollar.) Base or standard pay accounted for about 27 percent of the total monthly income of workers and staff in this plant, and it is in the complex increments to the base pay that a further understanding of the Japanese factory's reward system lies.

This plant, and it is typical, pays a series of additional allowances, based on factors bearing no relation to work performance or factory output, which comprise the larger portion of the worker's income. The first is the so-called work allowance, an additional 105 percent of base pay for staff and monthly paid workers and 125 percent for daily paid workers. The second allowance is based on attendance. Twenty-nine yen are paid to all employees for each day's attendance. Another allowance, identical for all grades of workers, is the family allowance—¥800 paid monthly for the first family member; ¥400 monthly for each of the second, third, and fourth family members; and ¥200 monthly for each additional member beyond the fourth.

A more substantial allowance than those listed so far is the age allowance, a salary increment based on age alone. The scale of payment differs slightly for staff employees and laborers, starting at ¥950 for staff employees 18 years of age and under and increasing to ¥2,750 monthly for staff employees aged 41 and over. For *koin* the scale begins at a slightly lower figure—¥750 at age eighteen and under and increasing to the same amount as the staff, ¥2,750 for persons aged 41 years or more. This age allowance accounts for about 10 percent of the total salaries paid in this factory.

The work, attendance, family, and age allowances by no means exhaust the list of increments to base pay. Staff employees receive a somewhat ambiguously titled "temporary," or "special," allowance. It is paid at the rate of 90 percent of the base pay of each staff employee. This scale has apparently been developed to balance the payment to laborers of a productivity allowance, which is determined in this plant by a seemingly complex formula: the worker's monthly base rate of pay is divided by 30 and this figure is multiplied by the "efficiency" of the plant for the pay period. Most of the larger factories, although conspicuously lacking in the time-study methods and detailed cost analyses known in the United States, have derived a base figure for "efficiency," usually referred to as standard output. When output exceeds this standard figure the plant is said to be operating at more than base efficiency; and from this estimate is derived the basis for paying the laborers a productivity allowance. Examination of pay records indicated that the output in large companies generally exceeds the standard output rate. Consequently, the large plants nearly always pay a productivity allowance. The allowance remains remarkably stable in amount and may be taken—in fact, clearly is taken—to be a regular part of the worker's income.

A further allowance is paid in this plant—a job-rank allowance. It will be noted that there is no provision in the above-mentioned pay schedules for differences in actual work done. Such payment differentiated by job is also calculated on the base or standard pay. The increment for the *shokuin* is from 10 to 30 percent for persons in "responsible positions," that is, for people occupying the positions of chief of section, department, or plant; for the *koin*, the increment for persons in positions of responsibility is 10 percent, and 20 percent for workers in very dangerous or highly skilled jobs.

Companies with several factories in various parts of the country pay an additional allowance. It is a "regional" allowance to adjust for differences in living costs in the different locations. A note should be added to this review of the complicated wage system employed in this metals-processing factory. The given figures for base pay are those for persons at the time of entering the plant—derived from age for laborers and education for staff employees. These base or standard wages are increased regularly, once a year for staff people and twice annually for laborers. The increase for staff employees can range from ¥60 to ¥390 monthly if the total base wage is less than ¥7,000; an increase of ¥150 to ¥260 is considered standard. The range for individuals whose base pay is over ¥7,000 monthly is from ¥60 to ¥450. The semiannual increase for the *koin* is ¥93 monthly and for daily paid laborers ¥2.50 per day.

An overall view of the net effect of this system of payment is given in Exhibit 2. It shows the amount paid *shokuin* and *koin* in total, by allowances, and the percent each allowance contributes to the total wage paid. As Exhibit 2 indicates, pay for overtime work is no small fraction of the total salary. Although it is not usually paid at premium rates in this plant, a 25 percent premium is paid for overtime work on production that is "needed urgently" and for work between the hours of 10:00 P.M. and 5:00 A.M. A 25 percent premium is also paid for holiday work. When shifts are used, the second and third shifts of workers are paid, respectively, a 15 and 30 percent increment to their normal daily pay.

In sum, the average staff employee in the plant is paid the equivalent of about $75 monthly; the average laborer's wage is about $65 monthly.[1] Since women in this and other plants receive substantially lower average salaries by virtue of their younger age, lesser education, and lower positions, these figures are somewhat deceptive. A comparison of the salaries of men and women in this plant shows that staff men receive

---

[1] The universally paid semiannual bonus is not included in these figures. (See pp. 107–108.)

Exhibit 2

MONTHLY WAGES AND TYPE OF PAYMENT

Type of Payment	Shokuin		Koin	
	Amount (¥)	(%)	Amount (¥)	(%)
Base pay	6,390	27.5	4,751	26.7
Work allowance	7,673	33.1	4,604	25.8
Temporary allowance	5,741	24.8		
Productivity allowance			5,028	28.2
Age allowance	1,835	7.9	1,982	11.1
Family allowance	956	4.1	1,367	7.7
Attendance allowance	678	2.9	693	3.9
Miscellaneous			367	2.1
Deductions	− 69	−0.3	−980	−5.5
Subtotal	23,204	100.0	17,812	100.0
Overtime	3,498	15.1	4,847	27.2
TOTAL	26,702		22,659	

about ¥32,000 monthly and staff women about ¥13,000; male laborers receive about ¥23,000 monthly and female laborers about ¥13,000.

It would appear from a comparison with recent government estimates that pay in this plant is well above the national average for manufacturing industries, which is slightly over ¥50 monthly for male employees and slightly over ¥20 monthly for female employees. We are discussing here, however, large factories of well-established firms, and only those where first-hand data was collected. Among the firms observed, the pay scale in this plant was in the upper half but was not the highest.

Wages are paid for a seven-hour working day which begins at 8:00 A.M. and continues until 4:00 P.M., with one hour for lunch. Overtime, which is desired and expected by the workers, is limited to a maximum of 50 hours each month. Sunday is the one nonwork day of the week, but many holidays are given during the year. For instance, there are 5 national holidays; a a week's vacation during the New Year's period is granted all workers; May Day and a religious festival day at the company shrine are also holidays for the entire plant; *shokuin* receive an additional 20 and *koin* 15 days annually; and paid holidays are given for marriage (5 days), childbirth (42 days), deaths of family members (2 to 7 days, depending on the relationship to the deceased), anniversaries of the death of spouse, children, or parents, and severe illness of close relatives (up to 10 days). Time off is also allowed for the performance of public duties and in the event of a calamity of natural cause. Although this imposing list of paid nonworking days is not complete, it gives a notion of the wide range of reasons for holidays. The working regulations are not, on the whole, onerous.

In summary, the worker in this factory, excluding holidays, works about nine hours a day (including overtime), six days a week, and receives about $65 a month for his efforts. The preceding paragraphs, however, do not describe the entire picture of reward and recompense in the large Japanese factory; and there remains an important series of extra-pay factors to be considered. Since it reveals much of the underlying rationale of worker-firm relations in Japan, it needs to be examined closely.

First of all, the pay system rests on the base-pay formula, which is not set by the kind of work done, the efficiency with which the work is performed, or the worker's capacity to perform his or other work. Base pay is a function of age and education, and only of these factors. Although some moderate latitude is allowed for competence and advantage, further increments to the base pay are primarily a function of length of service. In actual practice it appears that little use is made of the latitude in base pay increments, with pay raises almost uniform for each age group. About 10 percent of the total pay is a direct function of age and, since the work allowance is a percent increment to base pay, this work allowance too is largely a product of age and education. Indeed, the entire salary is largely based on the employee's educational status on entering the company and the length of time he has served. The exceptions are the family allowance, quite irrelevant to factory performance, the attendance allowance, hardly a critical test of job competence, and the job-rank allowance which alone is related closely to the nature of the work performed. In other words, only a small part of the total reward of the Japanese worker depends on the kind of work he does and the way in which he does it. This fact has far-reaching implications in terms of both systems of production and systems of human relations. Its importance is underlined when the examination of the reward system proceeds from the direct monetary rewards to the total range of rewards and incentives provided the Japanese worker.

Data obtained in another specific plant will be used to illustrate the further range of the system of reward and its importance in the total worker compensation scheme in Japan. This plant is a textile manufacturing plant which employs 3,500 workers, about one-third of whom are women. The average age of the male worker is 30 years, that of the women 23 years; the average length of service is about 7 years. Exhibit 3 presents the budget for a one-month period of the welfare activities carried out for the laborers in this plant.

An appreciation of the magnitude of the expenditure may be gained by comparing the net sum of ¥11,000,000 expended for welfare activities with the total payroll of ¥50,405,000 for the same month. The welfare program in this plant represents a 20 percent increment to the total direct labor payment.

Some of the items listed in Exhibit 3 warrant a closer look. First of all, the company provides meals in the company cafeteria for all employees during working hours, usually the noon meal, for which the worker pays ¥30 (about 8 cents). If he lives in a dormitory he can eat his other meals at a similar

Exhibit 3

MONTHLY BUDGET OF A WELFARE PROGRAM
IN A TEXTILE PLANT
(Thousands of ¥)

Type of Activity	Total Cost	Total Income
Meals	3,422	1,758
Dormitories	4,720	15
Bath	48	0
Company houses	1,225	187
Kindergarten	83	14
Company store	481	618
Schools	282	0
Library	54	0
Dormitory clubs	260	2
Park	66	7
Hospital and health	3,954	812
TOTAL	14,595	3,413

cost. Thus a young worker in this company can eat at his accepted standard for about $7 per month. His room, shared with others in the dormitory, which has a game room, dining room, laundry, and other facilities, will cost him ¥155 (less than 50 cents) each month. The staff for the dining rooms and dormitories are company personnel. The public bath, a popular institution in Japan, is provided and maintained in the factory area by the company at no cost to the workers. Haircuts and shampoos may be obtained in the company barbershop. The company store sells articles such as toilet goods and clothing at about 10 percent below market cost. Since the company maintains a well-equipped and well-staffed dental and medical center, the worker's medical expenses are almost nil. Athletic facilities exist in considerable number, and the dormitory has an extensive and active club system to provide entertainment. The worker is most likely to spend his holidays at the mountain or beach dormitory maintained by the company, for which he will be charged a small fee. In short, nearly every detail of his life is interpenetrated by the company's facilities, guidance, and assistance.

When a young man in this textile plant marries he receives other benefits. If he is from a distant village he will probably live in a company house where his monthly rent will be slightly higher than in the dormitory, probably about ¥700. His wife receives medical attention from the company clinic at one-quarter of full cost and purchases most nonfood items for the home from the company store. If the worker lives some distance from the plant his costs of commuting will be shared by the company. At the time of his marriage he receives a sum equal to about one-third of a month's wages from both the company and the cooperative to which he belongs as an employee. He will also receive financial aid in the event of illness, death, or other misfortune. His income increases with marriage, of course, and will increase still more as children are born. His children may attend the company school.

It would be tedious to provide a catalogue of the ways in which benefits and services are provided the Japanese worker quite apart from his directly paid wages. The intention here is to illustrate the kinds and the range of such indirect benefits and to indicate the involvement of the reward system of a company in the life of the worker.

In some respects the welfare program in this particular plant is more extensive than the average. For example, in an effort to increase the involvement of the individual in the company, management instituted a program of inviting parents of workers from distant villages to spend a weekend at the plant, stay in the dormitory, see their children, and learn about the company and their children's work. However, every plant observed had an elaborate program of benefits, varying somewhat with geographical and historical circumstances. Even in the large cities most plants provide company housing for at least a third of their employees. The benefits described are, of course, in addition to those required by law, such as disability insurance.

Before examining the social implications of the Japanese compensation system, two more aspects of the welfare program must be noted. The first is the retirement system used in the large factory; the second, returning to wages, is the system of bonuses by which the wage level is increased about 10 percent.

When visiting Japanese companies, conversation repeatedly turned to a discussion of retirement age and retirement pay, asking for information about and comparing the retirement programs of American and Japanese firms. The problem is a serious one for Japanese companies, one made no less difficult by the enormous inflation of currency in the postwar period. As is clear from the description of management attitudes, Japanese management has a considerable responsibility, extending beyond the workshop, for the workers. In this kind of worker-firm relationship it is not possible to simply dismiss workers with no further concern at the end of their period of usefulness. At the same time neither the Japanese business firm nor the Japanese government has devised any system of retirement pay or allowances that would enable the worker to look ahead to a secure living after leaving the factory.

The present average retirement age in most large Japanese factories is 55 years for male employees. The age, however, sometimes differs by employee rank, higher-ranked employees being allowed to work to an older age. The stated retirement age for women is usually 50 years, although in fact it would be a rare case in which a woman remained in the company's employ much beyond 30 years of age. The retirement age limit is strictly enforced except, as noted, with members of top management. Senior executives often continue in their positions well beyond the 55-year limit.

Looking first at the retirement system for laborers, the

practice in a specific company will be cited to indicate the kind of retirement allowance paid. Retirement pay in this company, as so many elements of the employee's career, is based first on education and second on length of service with the company. The company has established a base amount for retirement depending on these two factors. Thus, for example, a middle school graduate who retires at the company's request after 20 years of service (a most unlikely event) would receive a total of ¥600,000. In the event of death or injury forcing retirement, the slightly larger sum of ¥690,000 would be paid. Should the worker of his own will decide to leave the company after 20 years of service, he would receive the full retirement allowance; but had he left voluntarily before completing 20 years service he would receive only a fraction of the total allowance. Exhibit 4 shows how this system works for the different categories of education at three levels of length of service.

The general pattern of the retirement allowance system used in this plant is to reward length of service in increasing proportion with time spent with the company and to penalize voluntary retirement from the company at an early date. Retirement allowances are not large. If a worker who is a middle school graduate leaves the company after 30 years in its employ, he will be paid ¥1,713,600, the equivalent of about five years' salary. It is not a small sum, but is hardly sufficient to maintain the worker and his family from the time of retirement to death. It is, however, a lump sum payment. As such it represents a very considerable capital amount and is often invested in a house, some part of which is then sublet, or in a small shop. The worker, however, must anticipate looking for temporary and part-time employment following his retirement and dependency on his children for support in old age. Given the present Japanese family system, such support may reasonably be expected from children or relatives.

Exhibit 4

RETIREMENT ALLOWANCES IN A JAPANESE FACTORY

Education of Worker	Length of Service (Years)	Amount of Retirement Allowance (Thousands of ¥)		
		Company's Request	Injury or Death	Worker's Request
University	5	64	64	32
	10	174	183	122
	20	960	1,104	960
Higher school	5	52	52	26
	10	140	147	98
	20	720	828	720
Middle school	5	43	43	22
	10	120	126	84
	20	600	690	600
Higher primary school	5	34	34	17
	10	92	97	64
	20	414	476	414

The foregoing discussion has been in terms of workers. Formally, management retirement is similar, and it will be noted that the scale of retirement pay offers no provision beyond the influence of education in the retirement allowance for job rank. Informally, however, a further provision is available for more favored workers and for members of management. This is the system of affiliated or subordinate companies whereby a large plant has a group of satellite plants closely associated with it. The subsidiary firms often use machinery and methods drawn from the parent firm and are dependent on the parent firm for capital and for business. The management of these smaller plants as well as the supervisory staff is frequently made up largely of persons retired from the parent factory, but there is no formal rule governing such an assignment. It is one of the points at which favor and personal relations have the largest play in the system of reward.

Thus far three primary types of reward and incentive have

been considered—the wage system itself, nonmonetary benefits, and the retirement allowance system. There remains still another tangible and important element in the reward system of the Japanese factory, a financial gain provided employees but one which is strictly speaking not a part of the wage system. This is the payment, usually twice annually, of a considerable bonus to all company employees. The amount of the bonus is often equivalent to one month's wages, or, during a year's period, an increment to total wages of about 15 percent. It is ordinarily paid at mid-summer and again at the end of the year, both periods, it might be added, being traditional for the exchange of gifts in Japanese society.

The bonus is at present very much a part of the regular wage system. Employees expect a bonus and organize their living standard around the payment of a bonus. Thus expenditures for special purchases, such as a radio or washing machine, are delayed until bonus time. Since its size is a determining factor in department store sales and vacation expenditures, the nation as a whole watches with considerable attention the bonus scale for industry for the semiannual periods.

The bonus payment for each period is the subject of extensive negotiations with the union, ordinarily over the total amount of money to be allotted for bonuses, with management enjoying the prerogative of assigning specific sums to each individual. As a result one might expect that the bonus would become a way of rewarding the individual effort of a particularly energetic or productive worker. So far as could be ascertained, there is, in fact, little difference in the amount received within given groups or by specific types of employees. The differences that exist are to some extent a function of job rank, and there is virtually no differential in the amount of payment within a job grade.

One function of the bonus payment in the Japanese factory

today appears to be its utility as a device for protecting from union negotiation the base wage structure of the plant. The complexities of the wage payment system are further extended by the bonus payment. Thus it is possible for management at a given time to yield to a union demand for increased compensation without altering the basic system of compensation. For example, the basic differential in wages between *shokuin* and *koin* may be left unchanged while some one of the several allowances paid, which are of course based on this differential, may be altered slightly. Or, again, the demand for higher wages can be met temporarily by increasing the amount of money assigned to bonus payment.

The system appears to be a makeshift even though it has become an integral part of the wage system in all large Japanese factories. It is an unwieldy device in all respects and has the disadvantage of requiring repeated and heated union negotiations at six-month intervals. The significance of the bonus system in this discussion is its essentially paternalistic nature. It remains, however taken for granted it may be, basically a gift from the firm to the employees of the firm, not an obligation or duty as wages must be seen. It should be emphasized that the amount of the bonus is only indirectly related to factory output or profit during a given term.

Discussion of the bonus and its paternalistic and nonrational nature in terms of the productivity goals of the factory organization brings up the related issue of management compensation in Japan. Since this study of social factors in management in Japan did not and could not extend to financial details, specific examples of detailed management compensation cannot be provided. To obtain such detailed information would have required an investigator with the training of an accountant and the instincts of a tax collector.

In general, it is true to say that the actual cash wages paid management in Japan are quite low and that the difference between managers' and workers' wages as paid in cash is not large. For example, in one large plant the factory manager received a salary of about $200 per month.

However, it would be absurd to treat this sum as his actual compensation. His home, a most attractive residence by any standards, was provided by the firm and cost him some $4 a month in rent. The firm also provided his car and chauffeur (a company employee), and may provide vacations for himself and his family in addition to a most elaborate and frequent entertainment schedule. Rumor and hearsay would assign a very considerable number of similar additional compensations to men at his level; and it is probable that the actual wages or salary paid are the smallest portion of the total compensation of top management.

The system of indirect and paternalistic compensation is, however, confined to the very top echelons of management. For instance, a young employee of a large steel firm who held no executive rank, although clearly a candidate for future higher position, received an income of less than $75 per month. But his five-room apartment, including utilities, made available by the company for ¥750 (about $2 per month), and the supplementary benefits he enjoyed made comparison of this young man's income with that of a person in a comparable position in an American firm quite impossible.

As world trade becomes more competitive, comparisons of wage scales between countries, such as the United States and Japan, become more common and more heated, but they should be undertaken with some caution. It does not, in fact, seem possible to directly compare wages in the two countries in detail. The wage system described here indicates that, on a purely arithmetic basis, the actual cash wage paid is only part of the total compensation offered the worker in a large Japanese factory. If a direct comparison on a dollar-and-cents basis were to be made, some provision would be necessary for the additional allowances, benefits, and indirect payments offered the Japanese worker. Another consideration is the fact that the Japanese firm, whatever its size, guarantees to the full limit of its financial capacity continued and total employment to all of its workers. This guarantee is a major part of the total compensation in Japan, but it is a difficult one to include in an arithmetic comparison of the two wage scales. It might also be noted at this point that, although the small Japanese firm, for example, a spinning company employing perhaps 20 workers at 40 looms, pays very low cash wages to its workers, its area of responsibility for these workers is very broad. It extends even to an obligation on the part of the manager of the plant to successfully arrange marriages for the female employees before they reach the age of 30 years. Here again is a real obligation on management's part, a real compensation for employment provided the workers, and a compensation not readily assigned a monetary value.

An accurate comparison of Japanese and American wage levels is further confounded by the fact that the worker in the large Japanese factory is substantially well-off in relation to the overall Japanese standard of living. When recruiting high school students, for example, it was noted that personnel departments tended to avoid city higher schools. Since the sons and daughters of a Japanese factory worker are sufficiently well-off in comparison with those of farm or other city workers they can and will attend college if they are able and intelligent. It is difficult to see how comparisons of management compensation in Japan and the United States could be made. Without being able to offer detailed evidence it does seem, however, that the gap in real wages between workers and managers is as great in Japan as in the United States.

An examination of the basis for the system of rewards and incentives in the Japanese factory reveals an important difference in the kinds of behaviors rewarded in comparison with the industrial system of the West. First of all, the forms of compensation are more varied and often less direct than those in American plants. Although American firms too offer benefits in forms other than immediate wages paid, these seldom go beyond such matters as insurance, annuities, and retirement allowances, which are only one step removed from an actual cash payment. Moreover, in the United States the wages paid in cash are by far the greater part of the benefits received, and it is the actual monetary wage that is used by the employee to estimate his worth to the company and his success at his job.

In the Japanese system, membership in the firm itself is no small part of the worker's recompense. Each firm has a distinctive insignia, made up in the form of a lapel button, which is a proudly worn badge of membership in a distinctive and important group. The difficulties of admission to employment and the nature of the commitment undertaken by both worker and firm at the time of employment find their counterpart in the less direct, less impersonal forms of reward. The company is held to be and considers itself reponsible for the total person, including his food, clothing, and shelter, and takes a direct responsibility for providing these things, along with such items as medical care and education. Stated positively, the Western system emphasizes the impersonal exchange of job services for cash reward. Responsibility for living and health standards is an individual problem for each worker. The Japanese employee is part of a very much more personal system, a system in which his total functioning as a person is seen as management's responsibility and in which his group membership transcends his individual privileges and responsibilities.

It would not be accurate for either system to describe the Western one as coldly commercial and impersonal, the Japanese as warmly intimate or mutually cooperative. There is a difference between the two systems, however, and the difference extends in the direction of these two poles. It would be no less accurate to describe the Japanese system as paternalistic or, as became popular in Japan after the end of the Second World War, feudalistic. It is a feudalistic system only by analogy, but it is a system in which the exchange of obligations and responsibilities inherent in any group interaction cannot be discharged by a solely monetary exchange.

At the risk of considerable oversimplification it might be useful to note here the logic that seems to underlie a system of payment in a factory where that payment is related only to the view of the factory as an organization to produce at maximum efficiency a given product. Reward in such a system would be given in relation to the capacity of the individual to contribute to efficient and maximal production. To the extent that the individual failed to contribute in an amount equivalent to another individual, his reward would be proportionately lessened. Payment would then be based on factors relating to the position an individual occupies and the extent to which he effectively fulfills the demands of his job.

The Japanese system of reward does not operate on these kinds of assumptions. For example, a prime factor in the payment system is the employee's age. Although length of service might be seen as having some relationship to job performance, justifying its importance in the scheme of job reward, age in itself would appear to have no relationship to the job situation, except insofar as advancing age might reduce job efficiency. This kind of nonrational reward system is more dramatically illustrated by the family allowance. Not only does the number of persons in a worker's family have no connection with the goals of the factory but also to reward, in effect, increased family membership seems a cruel contradiction in a nation painfully subject to a high population density.

In other words, recompense in the Japanese factory is in

large part a function of matters that have no direct connection with the factory's productivity goals. They can be termed relevant to factory pay only when the relationship between worker and firm, and the assumptions on which that relationship rests, are defined outside the more limited range of productivity, output, profit, and efficiency. It is not at all difficult to find situations where workers doing identical work at an identical pace receive markedly different salaries, or where a skilled workman is paid at a rate below that of a sweeper or doorman. The position occupied and the amount produced do not determine the reward provided.

In terms of factory efficiency two primary results obtain from this system of payment and reward. The first is the furthering of the limitations on the mobility of the workers. The importance given to education, age, length of service, and similar factors in the total wage scale means that the worker is heavily penalized for job mobility and strongly rewarded for steady service. What is rewarded is the worker's loyalty and a deep commitment to the firm.

In terms of modern production methods the reward apparatus has a second and more immediate effect. The whole mechanism of job evaluation, cost analysis, and incentive systems can find no place in the large Japanese factory without clashing violently with the present system. Underlying all devices for increased productivity is the assumption that the individual should be rewarded in relation to specified job demands and his individual work effort. It is possible to find in the large Japanese factory some measure of wage differential by job type, usually limited to some additional payment for extremely hazardous work, as, for example, in shipyards and steel forges. As in the pay scales cited above, it is also possible to find some recompense on a group basis for productivity. These two examples are, however, minor exceptions to the general rule that job output does not govern wage level.

More important, as has been noted, individual effort is not a component of wage calculation. It is seldom possible to identify and isolate individual competence or individual job responsibility in the Japanese factory.

In devices such as time and motion study the individual's skill and speed are under constant scrutiny. Although informal group pressures may govern the worker's particular reactions, the fact remains that his pay and his progress in the plant are partly based on and always susceptible to measurement in terms of his individual output. A thoroughgoing system of cost analysis demands this kind of precision in the calculation of output. It is perhaps not too much to say that in the American firm the underlying assumption of incentive methods is one of individual responsibility to which the informal group makes certain adaptations. In the Japanese factory, however, it is group work and group output that measure success, with only some minor accommodations to individual differences.

It is on this general point that many of the efforts to introduce new, usually American-style methods into the Japanese firm flounder. Japanese engineers and managers who attempt to introduce quality control and cost analysis into a plant sometimes find themselves unable to obtain the necessary information and support; American technicians fail to communicate successfully what it is they are trying to accomplish. In both situations the difficulty appears to stem from the fact that Western methods rely on assumptions about the nature of the work experience which are not valid for the Japanese work situation.

In attempting to summarize the general differences between the reward systems in the large Japanese factories and those in comparable American production units, it is apparent that the definitions of the work situation and the nature of the work experience differ. The qualities on which recompense is based in the Japanese factory are those broad social considerations—

such as age, education, and number of family members—
which can be seen as relevant to work compensation only if
the nature of the work group is viewed in a way different from
that in the United States. Membership in this work group rests
on general considerations of character and background. It is
a permanent membership. Reward is thus related to fidelity to
the needs of the individual as husband and father. Motivation
for work output rests in large part on loyalty and group identification. In terms of motivation and reward, the group operates
in a context quite different from that of the American work
unit, one more nearly akin to our family groupings.

5.

RANK, CAREERS,
AND THE FORMAL ORGANIZATION

To OBTAIN a perspective on the underlying nature of the social organization of the large Japanese factory, it is useful to look briefly into the surroundings and organization of some of the myriad small production units of Japan. There are revealed in these small factories, employing only a few people, elements that are hard to discern in the giant and complex factory units. In the small factory one finds the analogue and paradigm of the organization of the large factory.

Traveling from Tokyo by one of the web of electric trains that crisscross the Kanto plain, after about one hour's ride the traveler arrives in a silk spinning and weaving center, a small city of about 30,000 persons. The city is not attractive. Badly damaged by wartime bombing—there was an aircraft plant nearby—its buildings are painfully new and crowded together; the city presents a dusty, jerry-built aspect, quite out of keeping with its traditional setting and traditional industry.

This city is a major producing center for silk goods, not, it is true, the elegant and expensive *kimono* and *obi* of Kyoto, but "middle-class" goods of moderate quality and price. The center of the industry is a new concrete and stucco building, quite modern in design, located on the main street of the town. This building is the headquarters of the cooperative society, which was founded in 1899 by a group of silk factory owners to provide joint services for the marketing and distribution of their products. The society is in truth cooperative. One of the many paradoxes of Japan is that a nation famous for fierce loyalties to family and clan should also have a strong and still healthy tradition, which has existed for centuries, of cooperative banks, communities, and all manner of business groups.

The 750-odd factories in this area employ a total of about 10,000 women and about 1,100 men. The smallest of the factories has three looms, operated by the owner's family; the largest, the president of which is head of the cooperative, has about 150 machines and 80 employees. The typical plant, and there are many of this type, uses about 20 machines and has 15 workers.

The factory of Mr. Watanabe will serve as an example of these many plants. Built just after the war, it is somewhat newer than the average plant, which in this city is about 15 years old. (The oldest has been in continuous operation by the same management for 50 years.) It is also slightly larger than average, with 30 looms and 19 employees. The factory, the workers' living quarters, and Mr. Watanabe's home are all enclosed in the same compound; indeed, the three units are quite inseparable and form a single work and living arrangement. The visitor enters the gate and stops at the entrance to the home, where a member of the family inquires about his business. Mr. Watanabe conducts his affairs in the family living room overlooking the yard, which is not only a playground for his children and the family's pets but also the space for hanging the drying silk after it has been dyed.

The workers in the factory are essentially an extension of the Watanabe family. The 15 women employees are young girls, aged 15 to 22 years. They are from farm homes in the surrounding villages and their employment has been arranged between Mr. Watanabe and their parents. They live in a wing of the family, and special holidays and occasions are enjoyed by the entire group, both family and workers. Mr. Watanabe's responsibilities for them extend beyond those of an employer in a comparable small establishment in the United States. He, in fact, acts *in loco parentis*. He provides care, advice, and counsel for his workers and, finally—no small part of his duties as factory owner—arranges or assists in the arrangement of their marriages. The girls enter the plant immediately after middle school graduation, serve a three-year apprenticeship, and then, usually after two additional years of work, marry.

The workshop itself is a crowded, noisy, loom-filled room presided over by an older man, a foreman. There are other men on the payroll: a mechanic charged with maintenance of the machines; a silk specialist who supervises the quality of the material, its handling, and the designs produced; and a young boy learning the trade who acts as messenger and general handyman. Each of the girls in the shop is responsible for two looms, set facing each other, between which she stands at her work. The atmosphere of the shop is one of steady, rather rapid work, but at the same time there is a good deal of conversation, joking and moving around within the group of girls.

From the background of publicity and controversy in the United States one might well ask if this plant is a sweatshop and if these girls are slave laborers. In a sense the answer to both questions is yes. The niceties of labor laws governing wages, hours, unionization, and similar factors do not penetrate the shop with any regularity. Apart from provision for insurance as required by law and occasional visits by a government inspector, this is the exclusive fiefdom of Mr. Watanabe. The hours are governed by work demands and extend to well over 60 hours each week. The wages are low indeed, and consist largely of the food, lodging, clothing, and care provided as one would provide for a large and slightly improvident group of relatives. Nevertheless, the atmosphere is not that of a sweatshop, and the attitudes and actual relations among the people, at least in this plant, are not those of slave laborers. Relations are close and warm, and the girls have a most intimate knowledge of each other. There is little leisure, and the Sunday holiday is spent largely in small domestic tasks. The world is a most confined one, seldom extending beyond the factory compound. Undoubtedly the system can be and sometimes is perverted into a vicious and punishing sweatshop. Clearly it is not here, nor is it usually so. This interval in the workers' lives, the five or seven years between school and marriage, is part of the accepted scheme of things for these girls, an interval in which they are cared for and in which they work in a fashion not at all inconsistent with their backgrounds.

Men like Mr. Watanabe are common in this small city. He is about 50 years old and has spent all his life here, working in silk factories and training for the position he has finally attained. His success is owed to his training, to the president of the plant in which he worked, and to his present very hard work. He started ten years ago with four machines and is on his way to a most successful operation. The original four machines stood in his home and were operated by his wife and one of her relatives, while Watanabe himself was president, mechanic, messenger, and silk specialist. Since the silk industry has not prospered greatly of late, not all men who started as he did have flourished.

Looking at men in the area who do not yet have their own plants, it develops that there is both a strong desire to attempt an independent operation and a feeling that it is now, under present circumstances, nearly a hopeless goal. To begin operating a plant of the smallest size requires about ¥1,000,000 (less than $3,000), an enormous amount of capital for men in their position. Japanese banks simply do not lend venture capital to unknown and improvident men who hope to start new businesses. Their only hope is the avenue Mr. Watanabe took—to work long, faithfully, and for little money for a man who is himself the head of a silk factory. In the fullness of time and in exchange for long service, a loan will then perhaps be made. It will be a personal loan and the interest rate will exceed even the 12 percent which is customary in Japan. The demands will be high, and the borrower who cannot meet his commitments faces total loss. About ten men annually begin operations as newly born entrepreneurs. Few survive.

Here, on a quick glance and a hurried visit, is a sketch of a large section of Japanese factory units. The community which forms the universe of a group of such units, whether city neighborhood or country town, is small and circumscribed. From long interaction and shared backgrounds and experiences, the workers in the factories are closely related. A complex web of relations knits the owner group in the community together—apprentice years, financial assistance and mutual aid, and obligations of services performed and favors rendered. The workers in turn are tied closely to the owner of the plant. He is in a very real sense their father for the period of their employment. Their world is usually limited to their own factory, and the relationship between worker and owner is made even closer by shrine visits and holidays together.

There is no intention of arguing here either that the large Japanese factory grew out of these small plants, or that the differences between factories in Japan and the West are the result of an incubation period of the large Japanese factory as this kind of unit. Large factories have their own history and a separate evolution. It is possible to say, however, that the patterns and trends which are present in more obscure form in the giant shipbuilding, steel and chemical plants stand out in sharp relief in the small Japanese factories. At either end of the size continuum, from the plant employing only the owner's sons and daughters to that employing 10,000 persons, the social context for both kinds of units is the same. The backgrounds, attitudes, and expectations of the people in the factory contain similar elements, and the kind of organization and types of methods developed by and for dealing with these people have basic similarities. Thus, Mr. Watanabe's factory provides a useful backdrop for a detailed examination of the organization and relationships of the large factory.

Management of the large firm in Japan, like its American counterpart, will often begin an explanation of its functioning with the presentation of a chart of the organization of the firm. Although the chart is useful, it must be approached with some caution by one with an American background. Whatever its seeming resemblance, there are major differences between it and an American prototype. However, for examining the formal organization of the Japanese firm and for searching out some of the factors which have shaped that organization, the chart will provide a useful guide line.

Most large Japanese firms operate in several locations. The main office is located in one of the large cities, usually in a downtown area. Since the war there has been a very strong tendency for the main office to be located in Tokyo—near the government, near the sources of capital and credit, and near the centers of foreign purchasers' offices, always an important factor in the life of the Japanese firm. The main office is the center of the primary administrative units of the firm, and the several plants, laboratories, and sales offices of the firm are scattered throughout the country.

To illustrate the central trends which appear to be common to the large firms studied, the organization of a firm manufacturing electrical equipment will be outlined. The firm employs a total of about 7,000 persons, of whom slightly less than 500 work in the main office and the remainder in its two factories and research laboratory. As in the factories of this and most other companies, the units of organization of the main office include, first, departments, divided in turn into sections which are further divided into branches. At the top of the or-

ganization is a board of directors, which in this firm includes
13 men, 6 of whom are also operating heads of units of the company. Reporting to the board of directors is the president, an
auditing staff, and a legal counselor. Since the rules governing
finance in large firms are substantially less demanding in
Japan than in the United States, the auditors are employees of
the company. The post of counselor is in many firms an hon-
ored and honorific one filled by retired senior officers of the
firm. There is sometimes a considerable proliferation of the
advisor and counselor positions.

The actual operating heads of the firm, the men who are
usually in direct charge of the company, are entitled managing
directors. In this firm there are two such positions, roughly
corresponding to a vice president of finance and a vice president
of production in the United States. The correspondence is not
exact, however, since in this and in many large firms the office
of president is not an operating office. That is, the functions of
the president are largely concerned with political and social
relations and with representing the firm to outside organizations
and persons. The situation is not unlike that, familiar to students of Japanese political history, when the emperor was in
fact powerless, holding an exemplary and symbolic position
with actual control vested in a military commander. In time
the military commander, too, became a figurehead, with control
passing to a family acting as regents for him. Without dwelling
on the parallel, there is a tendency in Japan for power to be exercised indirectly through symbolic leaders. This tendency may
be noted in the large companies, where functioning responsibility and control seem usually to rest with the managing directors, as well as in the Japanese government. In some companies
the control function is divided into a senior managing director
group and a managing director group. In the company which
is being considered here no such further division has yet
developed.

Reporting to the managing directors in this firm are 13 department heads, including the heads of the 10 departments of the main office and the heads of the two factories and the laboratory. That is, the main office department chiefs have positions equal in rank and authority to, and separate in the organization's structure from, the operating or line managers, which would appear, in terms of presentation on a chart, to make for a neat separation of line and staff functions in the Japanese factory. In actual fact, as will be seen, the staff or main office departments run parallel to the factory organization, but the line of demarcation is not clear and is constantly changing. The rule-of-thumb procedure is for matters concerning the company as a whole to be decided by the main office and those involving a local plant to be decided at the plant level. The rule is not entirely useful. For example, both the main office and the individual plants have personnel departments. Promotions at the executive level, or above general foremen, are decided by the main office, thus extending the influence of the main office personnel department far into the local plant. Also, on a given local issue, such as defining the authority of a foreman in a department or settling the pay rate of a certain type of worker, it is exceedingly difficult to determine whether the decision is in fact a local issue or one which may have company-wide ramifications. The problem will be referred to again in terms of the whole issue of decision-making in the Japanese organization. At this point one should bear in mind the existence of the parallel plant and main office organizations.

At the level of department heads a distinctive feature of Japanese organization is highlighted. The 13 department heads in this company have a total of 19 deputy or assistant department managers. This proliferation of assistants and deputies with their seniors provides a total of 51 persons at the top level of management.

As in other Japanese firms the departments are divided into

sections. The main office of this firm has a total of 29 sections, with 22 persons serving in the positions of deputy and assistant section chiefs. The final division of the main office organization is the branch, with 47 branches of the sections. Nearly one out of three of the employees in the main office has a formal title and formal position in the organization—despite the fact that a very considerable volume of clerical, statistical, and accounting work is carried on in the main office without the aid of the many machines and computers now common in most American firms.

To summarize, there are three main features of main office organization. First, the organization is elaborately and minutely divided into separate, formally distinct groupings. Second, a very high proportion of persons hold formal positions and titles. Third, the complexity of the organization is heightened by the presence of large numbers of deputies and assistants to department and section chiefs.

The organization chart now leads to one of the factories, where just under 3,000 persons are employed. It is a relatively new plant producing modern radio-communications equipment and is in no sense old-fashioned or representative of regressive trends in Japanese management. On the contrary, it is considerably more progressive and modern than many. Within the factory there is the same division of staff and line as seen in the main office. This administrative and staff functions, however, do not have a parallel system in the factory or line organization. The two are formally quite distinct.

Seventeen administrative units report directly to the plant manager, his deputy, and two assistants. They include 5 departments, each headed by a department manager, with a total of 7 deputy and assistant department managers. Under the departments there are 20 sections, with 15 assistant section chiefs. The sections in turn are divided into a total of 78 branches. In the staff organization 12 section heads and 7 deputy chiefs report to the plant manager. These sections in turn are divided into 35 branches. Thus in this plant there are 183 executive positions above the level of foreman or general foreman, with four levels of management above the foreman level.

In general, the ratio of the number of persons in one level of management to that in the next descending level is roughly one to three in the large Japanese factory. That is, one president has reporting to him two or three managing directors who are superordinate to about 10 department chiefs. Each department is divided into about three sections and these in turn into three or four branches. Although the terminology for these several units differs from plant to plant, the general structure is similar. The one-to-three ratio of division generally prevails at the several levels of foremen, with at least two groups of first-line supervisors. The terminology here varies greatly, as does the definition of the position, its authority and responsibility. The common pattern is a work group of perhaps 10 laborers led by a group leader, whose job corresponds roughly to the role of gang boss in some American operations. Although this position does not usually carry formal responsibilities, it does have a formal title and rank in some plants. In a factory employing some 4,500 laborers, approximately 450 men would hold the rank of group leader or foreman and about 150 men would rank as general foremen, each with two or three groups under him.

This, in barest outline, is the formal organization of a representative large Japanese firm. The ratio of employees in formally differentiated positions to general clerical and factory employees is about one to six. Leaving aside the assistant and deputy positions, from worker to president in this minimal scheme there are nine levels of rank, which must not, however, be conceived of as a continuous progression. The differentiation between *shokuin* and *koin* discussed earlier makes for sharp division and wide differentiation of personnel in background and status between the levels of branch chief and foreman.

It is this division between status and role at the branch chief level that introduces an important addendum to the scheme in the plant described here. In a number of plants studied, where the component of technical training was of particular importance to plant functioning, an intermediate post was introduced between foreman and branch chief. It is ordinarily filled by young college graduates who, as a result of the recruitment and and personnel methods used, cannot be placed in first-line supervisory positions. As recent graduates from college, they are not sufficiently experienced or trained to assume management responsibility. At the same time, owing to their status when hired, they cannot be placed as workers. They are therefore assigned variously titled posts in which they act as technical assistants to general foremen.

The creation of these intermediate positions is a good example of the kinds of adjustments and accommodations forced on the Japanese organization by the nature of the worker-firm relationship and the conflicting demands of technology and interpersonal relations. An extreme example of this conflict is provided by the situation in a mine in Shikoku, which is part of a major metals-producing complex. The miners are recruited from the mountain villages near this isolated section of Shikoku Island. Operations in this mine were begun in the seventeenth century, and several generations of many of the families have worked in the mine. The role of tradition, superstition, and local custom in the actual mining operations is very great, and the men can be effectively supervised only by foremen and leaders thoroughly familiar with these customs and traditions. The young college graduates who will manage the mine, however, are recruited from the universities of Tokyo by the main office and dispatched to the mine area for a period. Although technically competent, these men are totally unequipped for supervision in these special circumstances. For example, if a miner should break a dish at breakfast he will under no circumstances go into the mine that day, believing that to do so would be certain death. Locally trained supervisors understand and respect the belief; young graduates of Tokyo's giant universities are less likely to be sympathetic. To make the personnel procedures fit the realities of supervisory demands in the mine, the company has developed a system of having two persons fill each of the intermediate supervisory posts. One is an experienced man with years in the locality. The other is a young engineer who may or may not remain in the local work situation for his full career. He must at any rate leave the actual supervision of the miners to his partner.

There are many similar situations in Japan; this is merely an extreme example of a common problem. The company is caught between the quite theoretical training of the Japanese university and the social demands of recruitment in the Japanese factory which prevent the staffing of managerial positions from the ranks of the work force. The result is a makeshift expansion of the hierarchy and the creation of an essentially redundant position, its functions and responsibilities poorly defined and its utility in considerable doubt. What is perhaps most important to note in this situation is the fact that the requirements of efficiency and rationalization of the productive organization yield to the demands of the social context in which the factory operates.

The complex and highly differentiated organizational system of the Japanese factory is of particular importance in two respects. The first is the effect of the organizational system on the decision-making process in the Japanese firm, and the second is the relation of the formal organization to the careers of the individuals in the organization.

In no respect is the difference between the American and Japanese firm more striking and the relationship between the social systems of the two societies and their business organizations more clear than in the area of decision-making. The elab-

oration of the managerial hierarchy in the Japanese firm has
been illustrated. What has not been emphasized is the extent
to which these formally distinct and well-defined positions are
indefinite and poorly defined functionally. The elaboration of
the structure in itself virtually ensures a considerable overlap-
ping of the authority of more than one person in any given area
of action. The problem of the differentiation of home office and
factory has already been noted. Staff and line functions are not
clearly differentiated, and there is a wide use of deputies and
assistants whose authority is ambiguous. Further, since the
range of any given individual's authority is not well defined,
there is a tendency to move decision-making responsibility up
the line of command. The consequences of these factors in
terms of decision-making are several. In the first place, nearly
all decisions are worked out by groups of people in confer-
ence and discussion, a necessarily slow and cumbersome procedure. Second, communication is not well defined, and the
levels of authority through which decisions must be transmitted
are numerous. Third, and perhaps most significant, it becomes
nearly impossible in this system to fix individual responsibility
for decisions or for errors in decision-making.

To cite a mundane example of how decision-making works
and what its effects are on the people in the system, the bonus
payment problem obviously has a considerable potentiality for
trouble in the factory. Since workers of any sort are apt to feel
discriminated against on individually determined payments of
this type, it would seem that the bonus might be a major source
of grievance in the shop. Japanese managers maintained, and no
evidence appeared to the contrary, that little or no difficulty resulted from the bonus. One might argue in part that the apparent lack of dissatisfaction stems from a general docility on
the part of the Japanese worker. It seems more likely, however,
to result from the system used in making the bonus payment
decision. There is no one person against whom the worker can

direct any dissatisfaction he might feel over the decision. The bonus payment—which varies but little from individual to individual—is decided not alone by the worker's foreman, nor by his branch chief, nor section chief, nor personnel department, but by all of these together with the final approval of the department chief. Should the worker feel some resentment it must be directed against all of these people, or, rather, against the company as a whole. And since he stands in a somewhat special relationship to the company, such resentment is neither easily mustered nor expressed.

This kind of approach to decision-making is not confined by any means to the bonus or wage problem, but is, instead, characteristic of all decision-making in these large firms. The advantages of such a system are considerable and appear to be rooted in Japanese custom. The tradition of family counsels, in which the entire family joins in reaching a decision about family problems, and of village counsels, where the village as a whole discusses and decides village problems, has been noted by students of Japanese history and society. The pattern has been attributed both to the close interpersonal relations obtaining within the limited Japanese group and to the special importance of maintaining status and prestige for the Japanese individual. According to this argument it is impossible to expose an individual to the hazard of direct individual responsibility for a decision. In practice, this approach to decision-making in the factory protects the individual's position in the plant. When a man must spend his entire career in one factory or company, it is important that his prestige and reputation and his relations with others retain their integrity. The decision-making system is admirably adapted to this end.

The system, however, has its difficulties, and clear ones, from the point of view of effective factory operations. It is a slow and cumbersome way to meet fast-changing market and labor conditions. From the point of view of Western organization it has the disadvantage of precluding the possibility of clearly fixing individual responsibility and of rapidly and efficiently correcting weak spots in the organization. The system clearly depends on the alternative goals. The Japanese choice is in the direction of the support and maintenance of interpersonal relations within the company at the expense of maximum efficiency. It is a choice which Western advisors, hopeful of rationalizing Japanese production methods, have special difficulty in appreciating.

The second area of special interest in an examination of the formal organization of the factory is the relationship between the organizational system and the careers of the employees. The organization comprises two distinct parts for the employee. The first is that portion of the hierarchy, accessible to graduates of the old-system higher primary schools and present-day middle schools, which extends from apprentices through workers and group leaders to foremen. These employees are *koin*; and the calculus of their careers is a separate matter from that of graduates of other levels of schools for whom there extends, at least in theory, the remainder of the organization to the topmost positions. In fact, career progress is more circumscribed for high school graduates than university graduates; but leaving this aside the careers of the better-educated persons take in these upper ranks.

There seems no question that the elaboration of positions in the upper reaches of management is partly caused by the extreme difficulty encountered in attempting to demote or fire employees and the need to offer title and rank to compensate for the limited flexibility of the wage system. Recalling the discussion of recruitment and compensation, it is clear that if an error is made in recruitment into the *shokuin* group some internal mechanism must be available to minimize the error. If a man is not an able factory hand he is not fired, but he can be shifted to some routine and harmless position without damaging the firm. Similarly, a man who enters the company from college cannot be demoted or fired. The need for some system of relatively harmless positions for the *shokuin* who prove incompetent appears to account for some of the elaboration of positions and titles. It is necessary to find a niche for a man of insufficient capacity where he can perform minor functions without too greatly harming the overall effectiveness of the plant and without damaging the prestige of the individual.

In addition to providing a safety valve for errors in recruitment, the multiplication of positions also makes it possible to reward individuals with tangible evidence of career progress within the confines of a single firm. The problem became especially acute following the war and during the period of postwar adjustments in those companies which had considerably expanded their work force during the war. They found themselves and still find themselves heavily overstaffed at the management level. To compensate for temporary losses of personnel to the armed forces, recruitment into management ranks had continued during the war, but both wartime and prewar personnel were entitled to positions following the end of the war. This fact alone made for a generous staffing at the *shokuin* level. Later, although this kind of war-expanded firm did cut back sharply its factory force during the 1949–1950 period, it was not able proportionately to reduce its management staff. Finally, the large company, while willing to cut off entirely the recruitment of additional laborers at the present time, feels that it must continue to recruit college graduates, at least in reduced numbers. The result of these factors is the presence in most Japanese firms of a very large number of management and staff personnel proportionate to those in laboring and clerical positions.

Apart from the need to reward able individuals, the pressure to provide career recognition is a function of two very general considerations. It will be recalled that wage differentiation is limited, and a title and the appurtenances of formal office are, of course, an alternative to increased wages in rewarding employees. Parenthetically, too, it might be noted that where one firm (or military organization or government agency) employs many titles and ranks, firms and organizations working in relation to it must also use a similar range of titles to facilitate communication.

More important by far is the second consideration in the use of title and position as career reward—the part played by age and age-grading in the Japanese company. The relationship between age and rank is a very close one in the Japanese firm. It can be generally stated that it is not possible to promote a man to a rank where he will be in authority over persons substantially senior to himself. By the same token it is necessary to promote a man to some extent when he reaches a sufficient chronological age. (Of course, since workers do not move from one firm to another, length of service and age are directly connected.) This general rule about seniority and promotions is true in both broad groupings within the plant, among laborers as well as staff workers.

Thus, for example, a group leader in a plant will have at least 10 and the foreman of the group 20 years of service. Progression within the management hierarchy is no less regularized by age. Age will not ensure progress beyond a certain point, but its lack will ensure that a man does not progress until his allotted years are fulfilled. Thus a college graduate will not achieve branch chief status until he is about 30 to 35 years of age. He will be 35 or 40 at his next promotion, perhaps 40 or 45 at the next, and will become a department chief as he nears 50. Not all will go so far, but age forces promotion within broad limits. No college graduate could remain without some rank indefinitely nor, conversely, of course, could he be promoted as superior to older men.

The importance of age-grading in the Japanese company

was illustrated in the one firm where a job classification system was found to be in effect. (Job classification, in a large and well-managed company, is an unusual device for a Japanese firm.) Five grades of workers were established: apprentice, worker, skilled worker third class and second class, and worker "high class." Further study revealed that this classification was solely a function of length of service, divided respectively into men with up to 3, 10, and 15 years of service, and, finally, the position of foreman, which in this plant requires 20 years of service.

Because of the overstaffing of *shokuin* in many plants, this general rule of governing promotion by length of service exerts continued pressure to have available positions that are at least formally higher in the company hierarchy. The deputy and assistant posts have been devised to meet this demand, but to say that these positions are therefore nonfunctional in plant operations is not to say that the men holding them have no authority. They represent, rather, a further division of authority and a further dilution of the decision-making function, which worsens the already present shortcomings of the Japanese organizational system.

This discussion of the relationships between the formal organization and the career of the employee is not meant to imply that informal factors play no part in careers or career opportunity. Some of the informal factors have been pointed out in foregoing sections. For example, nepotism plays a definite role in the basic recruitment process. In addition, the literature on Japanese society makes reference to a special kind of informal relationship, known as the *oyabun-kobun*, or parent-child relationship, that should be briefly considered here. It is an explicitly recognized set of reciprocal obligations between senior and junior that have been observed and delineated for certain kinds of Japanese work relationships. In the course of this study some attention was paid this kind of relationship. On the whole it appears justified to report that the *oyabun-kobun* relationship in its true form does not exist in the large firm. Certain kinds of industry, especially stevedoring and construction work, retain this form of organization, however, and it is a conspicuous feature of the considerable gambling and entertainment industry of Japan. Apart from these semilegal and illegal areas, it is interesting to note that the relationship survives most strongly in those industries which, in the United States at least, are most heavily ridden with racketeering; and the system has real parallels to American racketeering. It does not seem accurate to describe the relationships between people in the large Japanese firm in these terms.

It is quite true to say that relations between younger and older, superior and subordinate individuals often have a heavy component of what we might call paternalism, which has close parallels to the father-son relationship. Thus, for example, the Japanese foreman feels responsible for the well-being of his workers, quite outside the work situation. Family problems, death in the worker's family, illness, quarrels between workers on a personal level, the well-being of the worker in the community—all of these have been in the past and even now are important parts of the foreman's responsibility. However, this is not the kind of formal and organized relationship that is implied in the *oyabun-kobun* terminology.

Looking at the present situation, and thinking in terms of management relations expecially, a more important term than *oyabun-kobun* is the word *batsu,* or clique. In the discussion of recruitment procedures it was noted that groups of young men entering *shokuin* status together in a given year are recruited from a limited number of universities, which means in practice that a given age group on entry into the company's employ has had some previous interaction and intimacy. This intimacy from college years is maintained in the company by dinners, parties, and other informal activities. Further, a senior member of management, usually a graduate of the same university, will often become familiar with and associated with the careers of such a group of younger men. On the basis usually of common university experiences and background there develop in the large firms distinct cliques that play a very considerable, though informal, part in career progress and success. It is this factor that helps account for the frequency with which graduates of foreign universities have real career difficulties in Japanese firms.

The role of a senior member of management in these clique structures underlines the importance of such a person in the training system of the Japanese firm. The elaborate methods used in American firms to train employees at all levels for their jobs is in little evidence in the Japanese company. Training is largely a matter of on-the-job training, learning from seniors and superiors. Thus the new factory hand is placed in an apprenticeship system and his learning is derived only in small part through formal schooling. Job learning takes place in the shop and, remembering that the vocational school or commercial or industrial curriculum is not part of the Japanese school system, it is the responsibility of the senior worker to teach the new worker the methods of the plant. This situation is no less true of management. The absence of formal training operations in the Japanese firm adds to the close relations between worker and superior and increases the ties that knit the worker to the company in an essentially paternalistic relationship.

These ties, established within the sprawling formal organization, parallel closely the kind of relationship indicated in the small textile factory between the owner and his workers. While the size of the organization precludes the intimate knowledge of and interaction with superiors that is the central force in the operation of the small workshop, two types of relations which parallel the system of the small shop may be seen in the large firm. The first is the strong tie between the company and the worker described earlier, the lifetime commitment of worker and firm to each other, and the elaborate system of extramonetary obligations and rewards that have been developed in the large plant. The second is the intrafirm relationship between superior and subordinate developed in the clique system at the management level and in the apprentice-teacher and worker-foreman relationship in the factory itself.

To present fully the close parallels between the small Japanese factory and the large one in terms of social organization, it is necessary to move beyond the formal system and look at the role of the company in the worker's total life activity. The interpenetration of job with other social activities that is so striking in the small factory may be seen also in the largest Japanese factories. The large factory, like the small 20-worker operation, is an organization which has its involvements with the whole range of the worker's life, an involvement expected and accepted by the workers and one which bears on such important questions as the role of the trade union in the Japanese factory.

6.

THE FACTORY'S PLACE
IN THE EMPLOYEE'S WORLD

BOTH IN the minds of the workers themselves and in the actual functioning of the factory system in Japan, the relationships between workers and their seniors, and workers and the company, cannot be described in the limited and relatively impersonal way characteristic of such relations in large Western plants. An illustration of the personal relationships within the Japanese factory was provided by the response of several categories of employees to a questionnaire designed to determine their feelings on a number of points. The statement that "A good foreman looks at his workers as a father does his children" elicited nearly the strongest agreement from all groups. It is assumed that such a statement would be greeted with derision, or strong distaste, by an American factory worker, but the average view of the Japanese workers ranged between "moderate agreement" and "strong agreement." Without placing too great dependence on these responses, they do indicate an essential difference in the quality of the relationship between the worker and the supervisor.

Something of the nature of the further involvement and commitment of worker and company can be appreciated by examining the extent to which the company and its activities and programs penetrate the life of the worker far beyond the work situation itself. While he enters the company for his entire career and the system of reward and career progress is dependent in large degree on personal and noneconomic factors, the company also accepts responsibility and the worker expects a commitment far exceeding the specific demands of an economic organization.

At the most personal level of involvement, the close interconnection of the business firm with the details of the workers' lives may be seen in the problems that arise in the company housing facilities. It has been noted that most large Japanese firms provide company-built and subsidized housing for at least one-third of their work force, a proportion which tends to increase in rural factories. A metals-processing firm in Shikoku provides well over half of its workers with company housing. As is customary, the area is set apart from other private housing in the locality and all residents are company employees and their families. A particular problem arose here when the workers' wives grouped together in a financial cooperative, each member contributing a sum of money to a fund from which members could withdraw in turn substantial sums for the purchase of durable household goods and other items. Such a system is sorely needed where financial loans are exceedingly hard to come by and incomes are low, but the company now has a policy of discouraging cooperative worker financial groupings. Some wives, eager to purchase a washing machine or radio, withdrew funds heavily and ill-advisedly from the group bank. When several of the workers' wives were unable to make the requested repayment to the group fund, the other members turned to the personnel department of the company for recovery of the money. When called to the office, one of the husbands found his monthly paycheck reduced and his family budget reviewed. He then received some general advice on the financial management of his affairs. The important point to note is that wives, workers, and company were right to assume that the company, although it had no direct concern in the matter, would act in the situation and, further, that all parties concerned would accept the company's intervention.

Many similar instances could be cited. For instance, a factory in Honshu, which has a similar housing arrangement, is alert to a special kind of problem that it frequently encounters. As in many of these housing areas the relations between people in the housing area have a most immediate reaction on intrafactory relations. Although there is some separation of housing by rank in the factory, foremen's wives and workers' wives will sometimes live near each other. Relations have on occasion become strained when the wife of a worker was able to make purchases, wear clothing, or provide her children with music lessons—to mention some specific cases—which were beyond the resources of the wife of a neighboring foreman. This inappropriate rank order among the women in the housing area affects the relations in the shop. In order to relieve the strains caused in the factory by this kind of interfamily conflict, the company has found it necessary periodically to move families to different houses, trying to mask the reasons for the move.

In another company, management's most pressing problem from the standpoint of personnel relations and morale was the inadequate schooling provided for the children of workers and managers in its factory in the Hokkaido district. The importance of college entrance in Japan has been noted. Inadequate school training will very nearly preclude a successful career in later life for the child owing to his inability to enter college. To help overcome the disadvantage of the rural and isolated location of its Hokkaido factory, the company found it necessary to establish special schools to aid the education of its employees' children.

These problems of family finances, living standards, and education give an indication of the range of involvement of the company in the life of the worker. What is most interesting about these situations is that company action was not taken reluctantly or accepted grudgingly. Both management and workers assume it is the company's responsibility to involve itself in such matters and the workers' privilege and duty to receive such assistance and attention.

In the typical large firm the company's involvement goes well beyond even these matters. It is customary to provide a wide range of training, totally unrelated to the job situation, for employees and their families. Lessons in those skills appropriate to well-mannered young Japanese ladies, such as flower arranging, the classic dance, and cooking, are attended by well over 90 percent of the women workers in many plants. Sex education and birth control instruction are also included in the curriculum in a number of large factories. Somewhat alarmed at changes in attitudes and behavior since the war's end, management now also provides the wives of workers with a wide range of classes in homemaking, family management, and Japanese arts.

Turning to another area of group activity, the company participates with the worker and his family in religious ceremonies. Nearly all large factories have a shrine on the grounds and give a day's holiday to celebrate the shrine festival. An indication of the depth of this worker-company participation is provided by the annual shrine ceremony of a large mine in Shikoku. It is held at the beginning of the year, and symbolizes the unity of management and worker and sanctions the factory's productive efforts for the new year. As in most Japanese firms, all activity ceases in the mine and smelter for the New Year's holiday. The representatives of the miners, senior workers in the company, carry a large piece of ore, the first production in the new year, from the mine, which is some kilometers up the mountain, to a shrine at the base. Management and workers join together in prayers and songs at the shrine, where the mine and the workers receive the blessings of the priests. Three days later this piece of ore is transported to the smelter where it initiates smelter operations for the year. The ceremony is an ancient one, and in its ritual is symbolized the close nexus of relation between all personnel of the company.

Looking back now to the small textile factory operated by Mr. Watanabe, despite the hundredfold and more increase in numbers, when compared to the elaborate organization and complex technology that sets the large firm apart from its tiny companions in the Japanese economy, the distance does not appear to be so great. In large factories the managers cannot duplicate Mr. Watanabe's paternal and intimate knowledge of his young workers, and there is an increased remoteness and impersonalization from the close matrix of obligation and responsibility that holds the small textile plant together. Yet, looking to the large American plant in the other direction, there is more in common between the large and small Japanese units in the way in which people are related to each other and to the organization than in the American counterpart of the large Japanese factory.

Analogies must be used cautiously and can hardly demonstrate conclusions, but there is an inevitable analogy when trying to describe relations in the Japanese factory. Compared with the relatively impersonal and rationalized systems of production and organization of the large American corporation, the Japanese factory seems familylike in its relations.

It is familylike. When a man enters the large Japanese company it is for his entire life. Entrance is a function of personal qualities, background, and character. Membership is revocable only in extraordinary circumstances and with extraordinary difficulty. As in a family, the incompetent or inefficient member of the group is cared for, a place is found for him, and he is not expelled from the group because he is adjudged inadequate. Again, familylike, the most intimate kinds of behavior are the proper province of concern and attention from the other members of the group. Fidelity and tenure bring the highest rewards, and, should the group encounter financial difficulty, it is expected that all members will suffer these difficulties together. Rewards of money and of material are secondary to the total success of the entire group. And, familylike, there is little recourse for the member of the group who has erred in his choice of group or who is mistreated by other members of the group.

The analogy is unsatisfactory, however. The family conveys notions of propriety and sanction not appropriate to a factory description; the analogy says nothing of the roots and causes of the kinds of relations so described. Furthermore, the analogy of family conveys a feeling of static organization, stability, and continuity that is quite inaccurate in describing the Japanese factory. The factory system is not static, nor are the relationships in its units entirely stable. The relationships which have been described are modal and generally characteristic. At the same time, however, there are areas and types of strain in this system, strains which will in all probability increase in the future and force changes in the organization of the Japanese factory.

Generally speaking, the modal attitudes and motives which appear to underlie the organizational system in the factory are traditional ones. The system itself and the men in top management who are instrumental in shaping and directing that system are very much products of prewar Japan. These men in top management, now in their fifties and sixties, were born in a Japan overwhelmingly rural and only a few decades removed from its deep isolation from the larger world. The large firms they head often trace their origins directly to feudal merchant families, and the traditions and philosophy of these families remain an active and real force in the management practice of the companies. Most of the separate factories investigated during this study are the result of the introduction of new products and methods into the parent company at the beginning of the twentieth century. It might be added that, whatever the merits of the antimonopoly laws promulgated during the occupation years, their effectiveness has been rather less than complete and the intimate relations between the several companies once forming an industrial combination have been substantially revived—if indeed they ever disappeared.

In short, the factory organization and its leaders are directly and closely tied to a nonurban, prewar, traditional Japanese experience and outlook. Leaving aside the impact of changes in world markets, international relations, and technological methods on the factory organization as now constituted, there are, in terms of the people in the system, points of stress where the attitudes and expectations of the employees do not fit well the organizational methods and the attitudes and expectations of top management.

The problem of the young university graduates from Japan's great cities, who have only a remote understanding of the beliefs and customs of the rural employees of the company, has already been noted. It is a single instance of a more general problem—the considerable and seemingly increasing gap in background and experience between rural and urban Japan. Many of the large factories are located in rather isolated rural areas, and their labor force is locally recruited, for the most part, by the personnel department of the local factory. The management group, however, is recruited by the company's main offices in a large city; and the young members of management are urban trained and oriented. The Japanese organizational structure obviously requires a considerable and intimate mutual understanding between workers and managers. Since such an understanding is only partly available under the recruitment and promotion systems used in the large factories, in many of the rural plants there is a considerable gap between management and labor, with an apparently diminishing interaction and amount of understanding between them.

Looking at the large factories in the cities, there is further evidence of the differences between rural and urban workers and the problems presented by these differences. It was pointed out that large factories would much rather confine their recruiting of permanent employees to young men and women born and raised in the country. Their "nature," it is said, is "more stable." In this statement stability apparently refers to the extent to which the worker can accept without dissatisfaction or unrest the working conditions and relations in the plant. Enthusiasm for union membership is only one, but an important, example of the lack of stability in city-raised employees.

There seems to be in these types of tensions a broad area of stress between the structure of the organization and its personnel. Exposed to and affected by the many changes that have taken place in Japan at an accelerated pace in the past two decades, young, urban-trained persons do not fit comfortably into the system as it has been maintained. Dissatisfaction with the age-dominated approach to career advancement is marked and freely expressed by many younger men in management. Impatience with the wage system, both for its heavy component of nonfinancial recompense and for the weighting it gives to age and seniority, is evident among the younger employees. Management feels strongly that the ever-increasing pool of city-trained workers does not fit the system of relations now employed in the factory. This sentiment finds expression in both the training programs designed to inculcate traditional values and the recruiting procedures employed.

There is no more striking instance of the kind of tension and other strains caused by the lag between changes in the broader society and the present factory system than the role of women in the Japanese company. Perhaps more than in any other single area of interaction, the relations between men and women in Japan contrast sharply with those which have developed in the West. More perhaps than any other type of interaction, changes induced or accelerated by events of recent years have affected the role, attitudes, and behavior of Japanese women. The resulting tension is highly visible in the factories and offices of the large Japanese companies.

It is difficult to observe any accommodation of the policies or attitudes of the companies to changes in the broader social position of women. It is the firm and hard-held conviction of men in all parts of the companies—the personnel departments no less than others—that women employees will remain and should remain in the company's employ only until they are married, and that this marriage should properly take place at an age no later than thirty years. Mr. Watanabe in his small factory is in a position to actively ensure the marriage of his employees, either by aiding its arrangement or by himself arranging the marriage. In larger firms there is considerable pressure on women employees to leave the firm after they have worked for the company for some ten years, and the pressure is substantially increased by the fact that almost without exception the women employees will have no chance whatsoever to improve their job status in the company.

This problem of job status is not only a matter of performing jobs at the lowest level of competence or responsibility but also involves such less formal reinforcements of differential status as the preparing and serving of tea to male visitors to the office, the running of errands at the request of fellow employees, and the performance of other routine or even menial tasks. The only exceptions to these general rules governing the employment and the job role of women in the company occur in those plants which employ a large proportion of women. They will sometimes become group leaders in shops employing only women, and on very rare occasions become foremen. No instance of a woman in a titled or responsible position was encountered in the *shokuin* ranks.

It may be that at some earlier period in Japan's history the

assignment to women of only routine, menial tasks was accepted by them as inevitable and proper. Some women employees
appear to accept this role without difficulty. It is clearly not
true to state that all women accept their job position passively
and happily at present. A very great increase in the number of
women graduates of colleges and universities has been made
possible in the postwar period. The proportion of women seek-
ing careers in business, laboratories, and other professional jobs
has gone up sharply. In one company, where the problem of the
woman's role was looked at rather closely (a company quite
Westernized in its general approach to personnel problems), a
number of women's college graduates have been hired since the
war. They appear, to an outsider at least, to be outspokenly
unhappy and even bitter at their position in the company.
The company's response to the situation has been to curtail
entirely the hiring of women college graduates and to confine
its recruitment of female employees to high school and middle
school graduates.

The situation has obvious similarities to that in the West in
the first decades of the twentieth century. A possible difference
is the emphatic and seemingly unanimous rejection by the men
in these companies of any suggestion that women might usefully and advantageously be employed in responsible positions
by the firm. To support the company's position references are
made to the underemployment of Japanese men and the sup-
posed inherent instability of women as employees.

An examination of the role of women in the large Japanese
firm reveals something of both the kind of problems which
social change and changes in the attitudes of employees are
creating for the companies and the customary response of the
companies to these problems. There is a very strong conserva-
tism in these matters, and the characteristic response to this
kind of problem is one of denial or avoidance. But the pattern
of interpersonal relations appropriate to the factory as it is now

organized, the intimacy between worker and supervisor, the dependence of worker on the firm, and the immobility of the employee—all are subject to strain as a result of changes in the background and thinking of the younger and urban-bred employees. It is a strain that seems likely to increase.

Against this background of the visible stresses in the relation between company and employee, it is possible to discuss more effectively the question of unions and union membership. Without understimating the potential importance of unions in Japanese factory relations or the importance they have at present in the minds of the workers as a good and necessary part of the work setting, the absence of union influence and the paucity of discussion on union relations when interviewing in and observing the factory situations was a striking and disturbing fact. As they are presently organized, Japanese labor unions, of course, are almost entirely a product of the postwar period. They enjoyed an explosive growth in the early days of the occupation, and every large plant is union organized, has a union shop system, and a contract with a union. The most casual observer of the Japanese political scene must be impressed with the very considerable and impressive strength of the unions, a strength which appears to be increasing.

However, when one observes not the Tokyo headquarters, the political scene, or the histories and statistics relating to the union movement in Japan but the actual workplaces themselves, the union does not appear to be an important factor in the day-to-day job relations of the worker—in his relations with the foreman, in his interaction with company officials, or in his activities in the housing area or community outside the plant. The position of the union in Japanese factories is, of course, particularly striking when seen in contrast to the role played by the union in large American plants, where the settlement or avoidance of grievances indicates the importance of the union in the shop and where discussions on matters of factory relations with personnel department members, foremen, workers, or managers will, if carried on to any extent, inevitably touch on or center upon the union and its relations with management.

To give an example of the differences, no Japanese company was encountered where an equivalent of the grievance procedures common in American companies was in actual effect. Unlike the American contract, the union contract in Japan, although often lengthy, does not deal with the details of the actual working relations—defining the foreman's role, setting out the relations between supervisor and worker, and circumscribing the role of management in its operations. Further, while contractual in form, the union agreement does not have the legalistic implications of the American contract. Its terms deal primarily with agreement on the existence of the union, its relations with the workers, and on wages and hours. It is a flexible document, indeed. In some companies it is subject to quarterly review, which, in effect, means that wages, the primary concern of the agreement, are under continual negotiation. The bonus payment, which is negotiated semiannually, also provides a periodic crisis in union relations. In conversations with the men in management there was no indication of a real or deep concern over the union's present or potential strength in the shop.

At the same time it would be incorrect to state that the average factory worker is indifferent to or unaware of the labor union. The responses to questionnaire items dealing with labor unions revealed quite general feelings that unions are necessary, not too powerful at present, and that they must be continued at least at their present level of strength.

The uncertain and limited role of the union in the actual workplace seems to derive from two factors: first, the history and leadership of the union and, second, the relationship between worker and company, which, so long as it is successfully maintained, allows little scope for an active local union. This study was not concerned with Japanese labor unions except as they appeared to be a factor in the local factory situation. For detailed and thorough reviews of the Japanese trade union movement reference should be made to the several historical studies available.

Looking only at the local situation, an indication of the inexperience of union leadership is gained from the history of the first postwar negotiation in a single factory. During the liberal atmosphere of the 1920's, this plant had an independent trade union. Although opposed first by a company union and later by increasingly nationalistic and rightist company-supported organizations, it survived until the depression days of 1931. No independent union existed from that time until the immediate postwar period when Japan became aware of the positive attitude of the occupation authorities toward labor unions. With the promulgation of the occupation directives governing labor unions, local organizations and national union groups appeared. The management of this plant became aware of the existence of a local group when three representatives of the local called on the factory manager early on New Year's Day, 1946. The union men presented three demands: first, that democratic practices be initiated in the plant; second, that the union be recognized; and, third, that wages in the plant be doubled. Since the first demand was sufficiently general and the second sufficiently reasonable, under the circumstances they presented no difficulties for agreement. The third, an immediate twofold increase in wages was another matter. Agreement was finally reached on a 20 percent increase, management reporting that this was apparently a palatable solution because the Japanese word for two times, *nibai*, is similar to the word for 20 percent, *niwari*. Management at least claims that the similarity was sufficient to allow the union leaders to retreat from the excessive enthusiasm of their first demand. Whatever the merits of this story, the abruptness of union development and the absence of a leadership with experience and training are illustrated by the anecdote. Although some number of nationally known individuals could be and were mustered to direct trade unions in terms of national policy and politics, there seems not yet to have appeared in local unions the kind of experienced and dedicated leadership necessary to solidify its position in the local work situation.

Regardless of the leadership available, however, there is little room in the customary system of relations in the large Japanese factory for a strong local union, that is, apart from the wage problem. The wretched wages paid in many industries and factories have led to some spectacular and bitter strikes in the postwar period to raise the wage level. In those plants studied where the wage level was at least the national average, there appeared to be a very slight connection between rank-and-file union membership and the large national union. Further, it might be noted that in the factories of the large firms with a standard pay level it is fairly common for the unions at each of the company's several plants to group together in a single organization not otherwise affiliated with a labor organization. Insofar as the gap between management and the workers, as, for example, the difference in background and training between newly hired *koin* and *shokuin*, continues to increase, it appears that the union will come to play an important part in the local situation. In the Japanese system as now constituted, there is little room for a union when the system is functioning effectively. The loyalty the system compels and the intimacy of the system leave little room for allegiance to still a third party in the actual workplace. The workers in the large firms see the union as a potential counterbalance to the excessive employment by management of its prerogatives. When seen from the point of view of the local work situation, the position of the national trade union in Japan appears not unlike that of the federal government in the United States—a third party in the work situation, not properly active but essentially friendly to the workers and a force necessary to curb the free play of management's actions.

In considering the potential of the union in the local situation a further point should be made. Although the weakness at the local level may be caused by the lack of effective leadership, the promotion system now in general use in the factories may well make such leadership available to the unions in the future. As a general rule, with but very few and conspicuous exceptions, ambitious young men who are sons of a laborer or farmer and educated only to the middle school level have no chance to realize their ambitions in the employ of the company. It appears likely that such young men will look to a career in the union, or a political career with union support, as a channel for their hopes and ambitions. Not only does management deprive itself of able leaders by its policies of recruitment and promotion but also it may supply antagonistic leadership to the local union.

7.

CONTINUITY AND CHANGE
IN JAPANESE INDUSTRY

THUS FAR efforts to promote industrialization in non–Western societies have been devoted largely to problems of assistance and change in the areas of finance and technology. The results of these efforts have drawn attention to the importance of social organization and of patterns of social interaction to the process of economic change, and emphasize the need for a further understanding of the interaction between technology and human relations for effective economic development.

Japan's extraordinary history of industrialization remains a unique record of effective social change, compelling the attention of those concerned with problems of industrialization and and economic development in non–Western societies. Japan strode from hard-held Asian insularity to a central role in world industry, world trade, and world power relations in a single, explosive burst of energy and remains the singular case of non-Western industrialization. The outlines of the story are familiar; its implications for present attempts to bring about development effectively in other countries are evident.

Yet there are gaps in available knowledge of the process as it took place in Japan, areas in which evidence on critical issues in Japan's transition is inadequate or contradictory. What particular changes were central to the transition; what elements of the total structure changed; what drives and needs made it possible for Japan to utilize the knowledge and skills of the West where other nations could or did not; and what kinds of people were the leaders, the men who turned away from traditional modes and directed the changes? It is in the answers to these questions that helpful insights might be found for present work in other societies.

The general view of Japan's economic transition is that the changes in Japanese society were revolutionary and entire. Far from being confined to those more superficial matters of habit, dress, and taste that peoples customarily find rather easy to adjust, they are held to have cut deep into the very roots of the nation's social system. Levy states, for example, that:

> The changes were revolutionary as far as the social structure of the society was concerned, and industrialization of a marked degree, far beyond anyone's expectations in the West, was achieved in a very short time. It is perhaps doubtful that any society ever carried out such marked changes so quickly and with so little violence. Land tenure, education, production and consumption systems, political systems—virtually everything—either changed or had its position in the total structure changed radically.[1]

What impressed observers of the transition in Japan was more than the extensive effects and the great speed of change. Germany too had moved toward a thorough industrialization very rapidly not long before Japan's singular adventure was undertaken. Germany, however, is of the West, the very birthplace of those attitudes and actions held to be an essential part of the process, as, for example, the Protestant world view. Japan's transition began from what was in most respects a greatly different

---

[1]Marion J. Levy, Jr., "Contrasting Factors in the Modernization of China and Japan," in *Economic Growth: Brazil, India, Japan*, ed. by Simon Kuznets, Wilbert E. Moore, and Joseph J. Spengler (Durham: Duke University Press, 1955), pp. 532–533.

historical and social setting. It then seemed that, in order to accomplish an effective and lasting transition, Japan would need to change rapidly in respects other than technology. As early as 1915, in a characteristic turn of phrase, Thorstein Veblen stated the general implications of this picture of revolutionary technological change for social relationships and for attitudes and motives of the Japanese:

> It should, then, confidently be presumed that, as Japan has with great facility and effect taken over the occidental state of the industrial arts, so should its population be due, presently and expeditiously, to fall in with the peculiar habits of thought that make the faults and qualities of the western culture—the spiritual outlook and the principles of conduct and ethical values that have been induced by the exacting discipline of this same state of the industrial arts among the technologically more advanced and mature of the western peoples.[1]

In the interval since Veblen's presumption, the view of a close and even necessary connection between certain kinds of social systems and industrialization has been much strengthened. A series of polarities has been put forth to indicate the directions of social change, change in attitudes and social interaction, upon which change to an industrial society is held to depend. Each describes an element of a general shift in the basis of social interaction assumed necessary to the change from a preindustrial to an industrial society. The view that the outcome of industrialization would be parallel for the social system of Japan and that of the West is set forth in Lockwood's careful study of Japanese economic development:

> In the traditional East, as formerly in the West, the Indus-

---

[1]Thorstein Veblen, "The Opportunity of Japan," in *Essays in Our Changing Order*, ed. by Leon Ardzrooni (New York: The Viking Press, 1943), p. 254.

trial Revolution requires a revolution in social and political arrangements no less than in production technology. Steam and steel, joint-stock finance, and laboratory science can transform the economic life of any backward area. Yet they are only tools at best. Their successful application necessitates a whole pattern of pervasive, interlocking changes in traditional societies. They can only be put to work within a new social setting which entails a radical break with the past, led by new elements in the society who will reject the sanctity of old ways and understand the social prerequisites of the new technology.[1]

These propositions argue that economic development, in Japan and elsewhere, is dependent on a series of changes quite outside the area of finance and technology, changes in at least two broad sectors of the society. First, an issue susceptible of historical examination, the process will require a group of leaders from outside the strata that produced preindustrial leadership. Second, effective economic development will be accompanied by profound changes in the social structure, changes eventuating in patterns of interaction quite like those evolved in the West through the Industrial Revolution.

On the first of these issues, that of the leadership of Japan's industrialization, opinions differ. Central roles in the leadership of politics and industry during Japan's transition have been assigned those lesser nobility who under the feudal regime suffered a loss of economic status and who held but little power or influence before the transition period.[2] Again, the merchants of Japan, enjoying great wealth but deprived by feudal law of commensurate social status, have been seen as central figures

[1]William W. Lockwood, *The Economic Development of Japan: Growth and Structural Change, 1868–1938* (Princeton: Princeton University Press, 1954), p. 499.

[2]George B. Sansom, *The Western World and Japan: A Study in the Interaction of European and Asiatic Cultures* (New York: Alfred A. Knopf, 1950).

in the changes.[1] A study of the early period of change assigns an important role to the peasants.[2] Still another view has been offered:

> The ease with which the transition was accomplished owes much not only to vigorous and imaginative leadership, but also to the fact that the political revolution represented merely a re-distribution of power within the governing class rather than an upheaval destructive of the old society. Consequently Japan carried into the new era traditional sentiments and loyalties which permitted her to undergo immense material changes without the loss of social cohesion. Even high officials of the Shogunate did not usually feel themselves precluded, on the overthrow of the old order, from serving under the new Imperial regime, which was thus able to recruit many able bureaucrats trained in the business of government.[3]

There is, then, an unresolved question concerning the kinds of people who led the Japanese move to industrialization, their social origins, and whether in fact the change in leadership through this period was revolutionary in nature. The proposition that these new elements of leadership represented a break with the past might better be restated to indicate the underlying continuity that accompanied alterations in elite groups. It would be of considerable interest in terms of understanding Japan's experience, and of some importance to the better understanding of the process of change in other nations, to have available a thorough analysis of this leadership group in Japan.

Of more fundamental importance than the question of lead-

---

[1]Levy, *op. cit.*

[2]Thomas C. Smith, *Political Change and Industrial Development in Japan: Government Enterprise, 1868–1880* (Stanford: Stanford University Press, 1955).

[3]G. C. Allen, and Audrey G. Donnithorne, *Western Enterprise in Far Eastern Development* (New York: The Macmillan Company, 1954), p. 188.

ership of the transition is that concerning the degree of continuity or discontinuity in social structure and systems of social interaction from the preindustrial society to industrialization. The assumption is that industrial development on the Western model requires a social setting radically different in nature from preindustrial relationships, a system fundamentally akin to that which developed in the West. The problem is no less complex than it is important. It would be presumptuous, with the limited knowledge of Japan's social system now available, to state the answer for the Japanese case to the general proposition. Still the results of this study of the large Japanese factory bear on this issue.

It might be assumed that, more than any other institution, the large manufacturing plant would represent in its social organization the extreme accommodation of Japanese systems of organization to the demands of industrial technology. Differences in organization, retaining similarities to earlier forms, might persist in rural social groupings and not be directly relevant to this question of the connections between social change and economic change. However, such lags in adaptation would presumably be minimized in the large factory.

In the foregoing chapters a general examination of several areas of the organization of the large Japanese factory has been undertaken. The area dealt with and the detail of the study are hardly exhaustive; it may still be possible on their review broadly to make out differences between the usual American factory organization and that common in the large factories of Japan, and to make some general statement of the nature of the differences. Leaving aside exceptions and details, some general features of the Japanese organization might be summarized.

1. Membership in the Japanese productive group is a permanent and irrevocable membership. Workers at all levels of the factory customarily work in but one company. They

spend their entire career in that single firm which is entered immediately on completing their education. The firm will continue to provide the worker's income at whatever disadvantage to itself, and the worker will continue in the company's employ despite possible advantage in moving to another firm.

2. Recruitment into the productive group is based on personal qualities without reference to a particular work task or set of skills. Selection is based primarily on the individual's education, character, and general background. Inadequacy or incompetence shown subsequent to selection are not a basis for dismissal from the group.

3. Status in the group is a continuation and extension of status held in the society at the time of entrance to the group. The broad dichotomy of employees into *koin* and *shokuin* limits the movement of an individual in the factory system largely to the general category that his education entitled him to enter on recruitment.

4. Reward in the productive group is only partly in the form of money, and is based on broad social criteria rather than on production criteria. The recompense of workers is made up of such items as housing, food, and personal services, with the actual cash pay of the worker forming only part of the total. Pay is based primarily on age, education, length of service, and family size, with job rank or competence only a small part of the criteria for determining work reward.

5. The formal organization of the factory is elaborated in a wide range and considerable number of formal positions. Formal rank and title in the hierarchy are well defined, but authority and responsibility of ranks are not. Partly in consequence, the decision-making function is exercised by groups of persons, but responsibility for the decisions is not assigned to individuals.

6. The penetration of the company into the nonbusiness activities of the worker and the responsibility taken by the company for the worker are extensive. Management is involved in such diverse and intimate matters as the worker's personal finances, the education of his children, religious activities, and the training of the worker's wife. The company is responsible for the continued well-being of the worker and his family, and this responsibility is carried out both in formal personnel procedures and in the informal relations between the worker and supervisor.

If a single conclusion were to be drawn from this study it would be that the development of industrial Japan has taken place with much less change from the kinds of social organization and social relations of preindustrial or nonindustrial Japan than would be expected from the Western model of the growth of an industrial society. The rise and development of the industrial West is generally attributed in some considerable part to the development of an impersonalized and rationalized view of the world and of relations with others. Emphasis on individuality, the view of the workplace as a purely economic grouping clearly differentiated in goals and relationships from other areas of social interaction, the subordination of other values and interests of the economic goal in business activity, the use of money to discharge obligations for services in the business world—all these and related trends are seen as critical to the successful development of large-scale industry. In sociological theory some of these tendencies have been set forth in polarities to indicate the nature of the differences. Thus, for example, "status" and "contract" have been contrasted as indicating the difference and direction of development with industrialization from a close, intimate personal group to the more rationalized and impersonalized relations of modern business. A more recent dichotomization is the differentiation of "parti cularism" and "universalism," or the move from a value emphasis on particular relationships and symbols, with stress on loyalty and intragroup harmony, to an emphasis on rationalized means-end relations, with stress on efficiency and performance.

These kinds of polarities are not altogether useful in discussing the Japanese case. Although it is possible to point to elements in the organization of the Japanese factory that fit the industrial and modern end of these polarities, a very considerable part of the organizational system remains more like the preindustrial pole. It does not seem warranted to hold that Japan is now at some mid-point in development. Such an argument is inconsistent with the view that contractual, universalistic relations are necessary to successful industrialization. Nor is it sufficient to say that, since Japan's industrialization is relatively recent, these divergencies from the pattern as seen and set forth in the West will in time mend themselves and fit harmoniously into one of these several categories without conflict or with few conflicting elements. In point of fact, as this report has attempted to indicate, the Japanese system is on the whole self-consistent. The recruitment methods and the incentive system fit together with the rules governing employment to make a unified whole. Change in one, as, for example, in employment rules, would drastically affect and require changes in other elements of the organization.

From this examination of the Japanese factory, the factory organization seems a consistent and logical outgrowth of the kinds of relations existing in Japan prior to its industrialization. The changes that took place in Japan during the last three decades of the nineteenth century are often termed a "revolution." That they represented in many respects drastic departures from the preceding period is clear enough. The manner of the "revolution," however, seems still open to question. At repeated points in the study of the factory, parallels to an essentially feudal system of organization may be seen—not, to be sure, a replication of the feudal loyalties, commitments, rewards, and methods of leadership but a rephrasing of them in the setting of modern industry.

It may well be that the kinds of experiences undergone by the West antecedent to the development of modern industry are indeed essential to an independent and *de novo* development of industry. The Japanese case suggests that these experiences and the organizational system used in the West are not necessary to the introduction of industry into another social system. From the observations of this study it would appear that, although the technology of modern industry was introduced into Japan, the factory organization at the same time developed consistent with the historical customs and attitudes of the Japanese and with the social system as it existed prior to the introduction of modern industry. Thus, looking beyond the modern equipment and the formal organization, the systems of relationships are more nearly similar to those which seem to have characterized an earlier Japan and which now characterize the nonindustrial areas of Japan than they are similar to the factory organization of the West.

Differences in the role of the individual in the Western and Japanese factory—the ways in which he is motivated, the extent to which responsibility and authority are assigned individuals, the kinds of rewards offered, and the behaviors that are rewarded—have a close relation to differences between the two cultural backgrounds. Japan's industry was superimposed in a matter of some few decades on a society that was profoundly and had for some centuries been feudal. The loyalty of the worker to the industrial organization, the paternal methods of motivating and rewarding the worker, the close involvement of the company in all manner of what seem to Western eyes to be personal and private affairs of the worker—all have parallels with Japan's preindustrial social organization.

This parallel does not underestimate the enormous changes

that have taken place in Japan through the period of her industrialization. Japan has changed mightily; and changes continue. If the study of industrialization in Japan is to be relevant
to the study of the developing economies of other Asian nations,
however, the nature of the changes which have taken place
must be clearly understood. What the results of this study of
the social organization of the large Japanese factory suggest is
that changes have taken place selectively—a point well remarked in other contexts—and, more important, that these changes
have been such as to leave unchanged the underlying basis of
social relationships. Rather than penetrating to the roots of the
social system, the changes have been built up from the kind of
social relationships preexisting in Japan.

A compact statement of the general nature of social relations
in Japan has been provided by Stoetzel. He states: "In point of
fact, as Ruth Benedict rightly guessed, the whole social structure of Japan is dictated by a concept of hierarchy deriving from
the kinship of the clan."[1] Stoetzel then summarizes his conclusions:

> To understand the Japanese social structure, three ideas
> must be brought into play, not separately, but together:
> (a) the idea of kinship, by blood, marriage, adoption, or
> service; (b) the idea of hierarchy, always conceived more
> or less on the *oyako* (father-son) model; (c) the idea of shar-
> ing in the protection offered by the tutelary deities, by a
> common cult or at least by a common burying ground.
> These three ideas are connected with each other, particul-
> arly the first two: wherever there is kinship there is a
> hierarchical relationship, and the opposite as we have seen

---

[1]Jean Stoetzel, *Without the Chrysanthemum and the Sword: A Study of the Attitudes of Youth in Postwar Japan*, UNESCO publication (New York: Columbia University Press, 1955), p. 56.

is also true; as for the common cult, it is the symbol of the family bond.[1]

Throughout this discussion of the large factory, parallels have been noted between the factory system and the clan or kinship organization. In terms of formal organization some of these have included both the manner of recruitment into the system and the kinds of reciprocal obligations thereby incurred by company and worker. Further, the formal system of motivation and reward has functional parallels to that of a kinship grouping.

In the informal organization as well the recurring relationship is modeled in the factory on the *oyako* relation, with hierarchical roles defined in terms of this pattern. This pattern is not, as pointed out earlier, the formal *oyabun-kobun* structure, but is, rather, an informal father-son type of system.

Indeed, so pervasive are the parallels to a kinship-type organization in the large Japanese factory that it is not necessary for the observer to argue their presence from indirect evidence. For example, in a 1952 speech to his managerial employees, the president of a large steel company said, "Not only is there the fact that our life's work is our employment in our company, but I feel that as people in this situation we have two occasions that can be called a 'birth.' The first is when we are born into the world as mewling infants. The second is when we all receive our commissions of adoption into the company. This is an event that has the same importance as our crying birth." Here are both a direct statement of the kinship basis of company organization and an indication of the way in which the common bond is symbolized, by treating the company, its history, and present organization as an extended family with common values, common ancestors, and common beliefs. It is for this reason, for

---

[1] *Ibid.*, p. 57.

example, that elaborate histories and genealogies of the large firms are written and that common religious shrines and ceremonies may be found.

It might be added here parenthetically and as a further evidence of the nature of these underlying relationships that the *zaibatsu* groupings in Japan are seriously misunderstood when seen as cartels or monopolies on the Western model. These are in a very real sense clans, the furthest extension of kinship-type relations in the economic and industrial sector. To treat these, by the passing of antimonopoly laws, as fundamentally economic and financial groupings was grotesque and doomed to failure from the first. It might be pertinent here to quote Lockwood again: "Too often in the case of Japan there is a tendency to apply easy labels, derived from Western experience. They may only obscure the complexities of the facts."[1] This statement does not say that the factory organization is "caused" by Japanese family organization but that both family organization and factory organization are components of a common social structure; and as such the system of relationships within each grouping has a common structural base.

It would seem from this study, then, that the very success of the Japanese experience with industrialization may well have been a function of the fact that, far from undergoing a total revolution in social structure or social relationships, the hard core of Japan's system of social relationships remained intact, allowing an orderly transition to industrialization continuous with her earlier social forms. It would in fact be remarkable if social change of this magnitude and success could occur in any other way. Discontinuity will not lead to effective adaptation; rather, it will result in chaos. The exceptional durability of Japan's social system, often remarked upon and demonstrated anew in her response to total defeat in the Second World War,

---

[1]Lockwood, *op. cit.*, p. 200.

is not the result of a mystic ability of the Japanese to adapt but, rather, the consequence of the fact that through change a basis for social continuity has remained intact. It is of some interest to note in this connection that the same wondrous ability to selectively take on new elements in a society is now being attributed to Indian society. But selective adaptation should not be remarkable; it would be much more remarkable if any people were able in one fell swoop to put off their past, their training and habits of mind and don successfully and permanently totally new social paraphernalia. Efforts to change the economy of other nations in the direction of industrialization might better then be concerned with an identification of basic elements of the preindustrial social system and with the introduction of new technologies and financial systems in the context of the older relationships, than with making these nations over in the image derived from Western outcomes.

A partial explanation, therefore, of Japan's rapid industrialization might well be argued to lie in the amount and more especially in the kind of continuity throughout the transition rather than in an emphasis on change. In this connection one might note that there is reason to believe that the pressure of the family system in Japan toward social rigidity and inflexibility may be commonly overstated. Although an analysis of the family system is outside the limits of this study, in terms of the thesis of social continuity and its effects on industrial change, it should be emphasized that in two particulars at least there has been within the historical structure of the Japanese family a potentiality for flexibility and change.

The first of these is the practice of adoption, by which not only more distant relatives but also able and promising employees and servants have long been able to assume important roles in higher-status families and in family businesses. This practice, not far removed from the notion of employment as seen in the large factory, not only has made for continual social mobility and flexibility even under feudal regulations but also may well have provided a paradigm for methods of industrial recruitment.

The role of the younger son in Japan is also of some interest in this regard. Under rules of primogeniture in a country lacking sufficient land there are provided the conditions for the establishment of an urban work force. Further, there has been a tradition of continuity, despite such mobility by younger sons, through the establishment of "branch families" tied to the "main family" by bonds of obligation and duty. The main family, in, for example, a rural village, under industrialization also provided a buffer against economic hardship and depression—an advantage still in a country where social security measures are meager.

These and other elements of the Japanese family structure, aspects of family organization conducive to adaptation and change, may well have aided the transition to industrialization by making possible adjustment within the older family system rather than, as is sometimes suggested, industrialization and urbanization shattering the older family pattern. Finally, and most important from the point of view of factory organization, the principle of family loyalty and cohesion, when successfully symbolized and incorporated into military, industrial, and financial organizations, may have become an important source of energy and motivation for the transition to industrialization. It must again be emphasized that such structural elements as these would hold change within limits, order the great transition, and prevent the kind of social discontinuity which would be destructive of a society.

Turning now from such suggestions as this study of the large Japanese factory might provide for an understanding of Japan's past, we raise the question of possible future developments in the organization of Japanese industry. There is a perhaps inherent tendency in describing an ongoing social organization to emphasize the integration and harmony of the several elements of the system at the expense of an analysis of stress or of present and future changes in the system. Yet in reviewing the Japanese factory the system appears to be stable in terms of the relationships between people in the organization. The organization is internally consistent and acceptable to its members so long as the membership is drawn from backgrounds in which the forms of relationships on which the factory is based are retained.

In terms of the people in the factory, two groups in particular seem to have some difficulty in adapting themselves to this kind of organization. Young Japanese who are urban reared, born in the large cities of laboring and white-collar fathers, educated in urban schools beyond the legally prescribed minimum of middle school education, and steeped in the impersonality of modern cities do not fit well into these factory relationships. Here is a central problem of the large Japanese factory. Workers born into traditional extended and close-knit families in the farm villages of Japan, for example, have, in the words of the factory managers, "stable natures." Products of small family groups of the large cities, unfamiliar with the elaborate systems of obligations and duties spun by kinship and friendship ties in the stable villages, do not respond to the appeals and rationale of this factory system. Women, too, who by virtue of family training or education have been schooled in a newer pattern of relationships and role expectations and who have come to expect an occupational role different from that traditionally assigned Japanese women, protest their position in the factory.

Changes in the factory organization may proceed from two causes. The first is prior changes in the organization of, and relationships in, primary groups in the society. The second is the pressure of changes in technology and production methods that would lead to organizational change.

The pressure for change is great, for example, to increase the flexibility of the work force to lead to greater adaptability to economic changes. The need for change has led, on occasion, to change in a limited sphere, as, for example, when a financial crisis and a subsequent "rationalization" movement led to the discharge of employees from a number of large factories. As in the case described in Chapter 2, however, it appears likely that makeshift and temporary adaptations which do not alter the general rules of employment and organization will be made. Real changes in factory organization will come about only when the point of view and the training of individuals in the system alter significantly. Thus the Japanese family system, under the pressure of urbanization, changes in religious thought and training, and under the constant impact of mass communication, may change the ways in which youths are trained and developed, thus changing the attitudes and expectations, motivation systems, and interaction patterns of youth. Although changes in primary group structures have not yet been carried to the point where the factory organization is in conflict with any major portion of the society's patterns of interaction, such a process of change, in large part the result of the growth of large industry, may in time alter the basis of factory organization.

It is easy here, as in looking at Japanese history, to mistake the nature of changes in cities and during the postwar period. The general formulas for the effects of urbanization have been developed out of Western experience. The almost total lack of close study of the nature of social interaction in the cities of Asia makes a prediction of the direction and kind of change induced by urbanization in Asia most hazardous. Further, it is far from clear at present as to how effective and lasting postwar experiments and adjustments may be in the Japanese case. It would be a daring observer indeed who would predict the outcome of the next two or three decades of Japanese events.

In summing up the results of this study, there appear to be

two broad elements of difference between Japan and the West in relation to the nature of the social organization of the factory. First, the factory, or company, is relatively undifferentiated from other types of groups in the society. In terms of the commitment of members to the group, the nature of their recruitment and subsequent careers, and the extent of involvement of members with each other as part of the group, the Japanese factory grouping parallels other social groupings. Although the factory may be defined as an economic organization with its goals narrowly defined and relationships narrowly based on productivity and profit, the Japanese factory is not so defined. The Western view of life segments, each serving a special end with differentiated relationships in each—the family, the club or association, the workplace—makes possible a clear differentiation of activities and organization in each group. In Japan, the factory recruits involve and maintain their membership on a basis similar to that of the domestic and social groups of the society. Where the economic ends of the factory conflict with this broader definition of the group, as in the case of the incompetent employee who will not be discharged, the economic ends take a secondary position to the maintenance of group integrity.

This lack of differentiation between the large factory organization and other social groupings is not only an internal one. Status in the broader community, as reflected primarily in educational attainment, is the critical variable governing recruitment and is the dominating factor in rank and career progress in the factory. Moreover, the employee shares responsibility with the company for his family, his children, and his general well-being. The broader social activities are not set apart from his membership in the factory or company.

Closely related to this latter aspect of the lack of differentiation is the difference between the American and the Japanese organization in the extent to which there is an individualization or impersonalization of relationships in the factory. It is perhaps this lack of individualization that most sets off the day-to-day functioning of the Japanese production unit from its American counterpart. The apparatus of modern production in the West depends heavily on the assignment of individual responsibility, on individual incentive programs, on the job evaluation of the individual employee, and on a system of rewards in which individual competence and energy will be recompensed. In all of these respects the difference from Japan is marked. Individual responsibility is avoided, incentive systems have little relationship to individual output but, rather, depend on group success, and the motivating of energies appears to depend on the individual's loyalty and identification with the group and with his superior.

In short, it may be concluded from this study that, although the preindustrial experience of the West may indeed have been the necessary cause of the development of industrialization, the introduction of industry into a society like that of Japan, which has not shared these earlier experiences and has a markedly different social system, makes necessary the fitting of the industrial mechanism to the earlier social system. What must also be noted is the considerable industrial success that is possible under these circumstances. It may be true that the Western style of organization maximizes productivity, but substantial industrial progress can be made within quite a different style of organization. Rationalization and impersonalization are not, the Japanese experience seems to argue, necessary to the adoption from the West of an industrial economy.

That the amalgam of a preindustrial system of organization and Western technology has created problems for Japanese industry is very clear, and some of the problems have been stressed in this report. It does not follow from the fact that problems exist that their solution lies in the direction of greater change toward the Western business model. This might be the case in some areas, as, for example, in terms of problems of sales and distribution where Western methods need not disrupt upon their introduction the ongoing organizational system. When other Western elements are introduced, however, whether by Western or Japanese advisors, the outcomes will often not be so harmless. Such introductions of new and Western techniques and approaches must be considered with some caution by American experts and consultants.

More relevant perhaps to present concerns of the United States are the possible implications of the Japanese experience in the problem of aiding the development of other non–Western nations. It would seem from the Japanese example that a considerable degree of tolerance—even at the cost of seeming waste—needs to be allowed local custom and methods in establishing industry in those countries with systems of interpersonal relations markedly different from those of the West. A lasting and effective transition to industrialization may be accomplished only when the changes are continuous with the preindustrial social system and are based on and grow out of the patterns of social interaction basic to the society.

Part III

ORGANIZATIONAL CHANGE, 1956–1966

In 1956 the Japanese economy, while fully recovered from wartime disaster, was still struggling to muster the capital and technology for a substantial position in the world. The next decade was one of enormous economic success and historic growth to a major position among the economies of the world. The stress of this extraordinary decade and of the social and economic changes that resulted provide a critical test of the stability and effectiveness of Japan's employment system. Far from breaking under the strain of change, or shifting to the Western pattern as companies grew and individual incomes rose, the employment pattern remained in operation over the decade with some strengthening of its basic characteristics.

Part III

ORGANIZATIONAL CHANGE, 1956–1966

THERE HAS BEEN a rather general expectation that as Japan's economy grows, as Japanese companies expand in scale, and as they enter into international competition, Japanese organization methods will move toward the Western model. It has been expected that job mobility will increase sharply, that compensation will become tied to output and efficiency, and that personnel will be treated in a more impersonal and "rational" way.

The period from 1956 to 1966 provides a useful test of this view that Japanese business organizations as they grow and are successful are changing toward the Western pattern. Both 1956 and 1966 were relatively prosperous years for Japan, and the intervening decade was a period of industrial growth in Japan seldom, if ever, equalled in any economy. Japan's gross national product increased on average about 10 percent annually over the decade, and industrial production more than tripled. Exports increased 15 percent annually, or nearly double the increase in world trade. A comparison of organization methods over this decade can thus provide a measure of the extent to which these methods are changing under stress, and the degree to which they may be moving toward Western methods.[1]

---

[1] The organization of large companies was studied in 1955–1956 (see pp. 53–171). (*continued overleaf*)

Companies in this Study

Twenty-five large Japanese companies provided a summary of their employment, compensation, and recruitment and exit practices as of year-end 1956 and year-end 1966. They are listed below. Each is a leader in its product area or field of activity. The range of business is broad, including a long-term bank, two commercial banks, a trading company, and manufacturing companies in product areas from consumer items to heavy industry.

The twenty-five organizations represent a significant share of the total Japanese economy. Their combined labor force totaled over 176,000 in 1956, and more than 260,000 in 1966.

Exhibit 5

COMPANIES IN THE STUDY

Ajinomoto Co., Inc.	Mitsubishi Shoji Kaisha, Ltd.
Asahi Glass Co., Ltd.	Mitsui Bank, Ltd.
Asahi Optical Co., Ltd.	Nichiro Gyogyo Kaisha, Ltd.
Fuji Iron and Steel Co., Ltd.	Nippon Electric Co., Ltd.
Fuji Photo Film Co., Ltd.	Nippon Reizo K.K.
Hokkai Can Co., Ltd.	Oji Paper Co., Ltd.
Industrial Bank of Japan, Ltd.	Shinetsu Chemical Industry Co., Ltd.
Jujo Paper Mfg. Co., Ltd.	Shiseido Co., Ltd.
Kubota Iron and Machinery Works, Ltd.	Showa Denko K.K.
Lion Dentifrice Co., Ltd.	Sumitomo Chemical Co., Ltd.
Mitsubishi Bank, Ltd.	Sumitomo Electric Industries, Ltd.
Mitsubishi Oil Co., Ltd.	Toyo Rayon Co., Ltd.
	Yawata Iron and Steel Co., Ltd.

This study reexamined, ten years later, some of the conclusions reached earlier. This report, as the earlier one, deals with very large organizations. Differences in organization that may exist in smaller companies compared with large ones are not discussed. This analysis was published in somewhat different form in Robert J. Ballon (ed.) *The Japanese Employee*, Tokyo: Sophia-Tuttle, 1969, pp. 99–119.

This was about 1 percent of Japan's entire 1966 industrial labor force. The sales of the 22 nonbanking firms totaled over $2,261 million in 1956, and $9,569 million in 1966, or about 10 percent of Japan's 1966 gross national product. Finally, the three banks represented are among Japan's most important. It seems likely, therefore, that any substantial changes in the organizational methods of Japanese companies would be reflected by these firms; they certainly represent an important segment of the total economy.

The impact of a decade of very rapid change and economic growth on the size and work force of these companies is shown in Exhibit 6. Sales increased for the nonbanking firms by an average of more than four times in the ten-year period, from about $100 million to about $435 million. Capitalization of the 25 companies increased nearly five and one-half times from 1956 to 1966, reflecting both the gradual improvement of financial positions of Japanese companies and also the very high rate of investment in new facilities during the period. The effects on productivity were dramatic. Against an increase in

Exhibit 6

COMPANY SIZE AND WORK FORCE, 1956 AND 1966
(Average, 25 companies)

	1956	1966
Annual sales, excluding three banks ($ million)	$102.8	$435.0
Capitalization ($ million)	$ 10.5	$ 57.7
Total employees, of which	7,048	10,415
Top management	0.2%	0.2%
Middle management	2.4	5.2
Male employees	70.2	64.4
Female employees	18.0	23.9
Temporary workers	9.2	6.3
Total	100.0	100.0

sales per company of about 325 percent in 1966 over 1956, the average work force increased less than 50 percent over 1956 levels. As a result, sales per employee totaled over $40,000 in 1966 compared with about $15,000 ten years earlier.

There were some substantial shifts in the composition of the average work force in this period.[1] While the proportion of the work force in top management positions did not change during the decade (an increase from about 15 on average to about 20), there was a sharp increase in the proportion of the work force in middle management positions. From a ratio of top to middle management of about 1:10 in 1956, there was a shift to a ratio of about 1:25 in 1966, suggesting that increased size of companies, and presumably increased sophistication of technology, caused a proliferation of staff and supervisory functions.

The suggestion of increased administrative and staff functions is reinforced by an increase in the proportion of female employees in the total work force, females totaling nearly a quarter of employees. On the other hand, male employees and temporary employees (presumably largely male) decreased—again suggesting very substantial increases in output by directly productive workers.

---

[1]To provide data meaningful in terms of Japanese company practice, and at the same time not make unreasonable demands on responding companies, this study used the following categories for employees: 1) top management (*yakuin*), which includes all executives at the executive or director level; 2) middle management (*bukachō*), including division and section chiefs, and assistant and vice chiefs; 3) male employees (*jugyōin-danshi*), all male employees below the section leader level, whether in white-collar or blue-collar jobs; 4) female employees (*jugyōin-joshi*), similarly non-titled and combining clerical and production employees; and 5) temporary employees (*rinjiko*), a special Japanese category for employees who are outside the system of lifetime employment, are nonunion members, and who provide some flexibility regarding total work force size, since they can readily be laid off on relatively short notice.

Recruiting the Work Force

The pattern of employment for large Japanese companies has been to recruit all personnel directly from schools. They are not employed for a particular skill, nor for a particular job opening. Rather, they are employed because their personal background and characteristics, and their general education, make them appear to be desirable and useful persons to bring into the company for their career. Similarly, the new employee makes his choice of job offers not in terms of the attractiveness of a particular position and its compensation, but rather because the organization as a whole appears to be a desirable group with which to identify oneself.

Therefore, a first test of the degree and direction of change in organization practices is the issue of amount and source of recruitment of new personnel to the company. Exhibit 7 shows the total recruitment into the work force for 1956 and 1966 and the sources of recruitment. The three sources of recruitment examined were:

1. directly from school,
2. from affiliated or subsidiary companies (*keiretsu gaisha*), and
3. from the outside job market.

On balance, the practice of recruiting directly from school was substantially more marked in 1966 than a decade earlier. For both periods, top management was drawn from within, with no mobility between companies in either period. There was only a single case not conforming to this rule—the fastest-growing company in the group of twenty-five reported that one of its top executives in 1966 was recruited from outside the company. At the level of general employees, recruitment directly from school accounted for virtually all female employees and more than three-quarters of male employees.

[179]

Exhibit 7

WORK FORCE RECRUITMENT, 1956 AND 1966
(Average, 25 companies)

	Top Management (%) (%)		Middle Management (%) (%)		Male Employees (%) (%)		Female Employees (%) (%)	
Total recruitment, as percent of work force	o	o	o	0.3	7	3	8	14
Of which, recruited from schools	o	o	o	o	53	77	74	91
recruited from related companies	o	o	o	67	o	2	o	o
recruited from labor market	o	o	o	33	47	21	26	9

A partial exception to this general pattern of continuing the unique recruiting system of Japan was the middle management group. While there had been no recruitment either from related companies or from the general labor market of middle management personnel in 1956, in 1966 a few cases were reported, still well under 1 percent of the total group. Eight of the twenty-five companies reported cases of bringing in middle management from outside the company. However, six of these cases involved sourcing middle management personnel from related companies. Of the few cases of outside recruitment of middle management reported, nearly all were by a single company. This company, the same one that reported recruiting one of its top executives from outside, was, as noted, the fastest-growing company of the twenty-five. In fact, its sales increased more than ten times in the ten-year period, and the company was a substantial one in 1956.

The suggestion here then is that the Japanese practice of recruiting directly from school, and not recruiting from an open labor market, remains very much in effect. However, there is some indication that at the middle management level, and under extreme stress, the large Japanese company can and does recruit from outside. There is little or no indication of a trend toward the free flow of personnel between companies that is held to characterize Western management practice.

Education of the Work Force

As the recruitment pattern suggests, education in Japan almost totally determines career chances. Point of entry into the company hierarchy, compensation for the career, and chances for a high-status position in the career are substantially determined by the amount of education the employee obtains before joining the company and thus the status level at which he enters. Exhibit 8 indicates how education and position in the company interrelate. Virtually all the members of top management of the companies studied had university educations. This is generally true of Japanese management, which has a higher level of formal education than management in the United States and far beyond that of such European countries as the United Kingdom.

Exhibit 8

EDUCATION AND COMPANY POSITION
(Average, twenty-five companies, percent)

	1956				1966			
	Colleges or University (%)	Higher School (%)	Middle School (%)	Total (%)	College or University (%)	Higher School (%)	Middle School (%)	Total (%)
Top management	91	5	4	100	94	5	1	100
Middle management	75	21	4	100	74	23	3	100
Male employees	10	23	67	100	10	37	53	100
Female employees	1	41	58	100	2	57	41	100
Temporary workers	0	0	100	100	0	1	99	100

In general the Japanese work force at all levels is a well-educated one. The high level of formal education of the entire

Japanese work force in 1956 was further reinforced by developments over the next decade. The proportion of workers with at least a higher school education sharply increased in the entire work force. Indeed, it must be concluded that the emphasis on formal education in Japanese business, with its implications for discipline, technical knowledge and work force adaptability, is a major factor in Japan's successful industrialization and present economic achievements.

Looking at recruitment by education, the shift over the decade has been dramatic. In 1956 over half of the male entrants to the work force of the companies studied were recruited from middle school graduates. In 1966 over a third were university graduates and more than half were graduates of high schools. In addition to the implications for improved quality of work force suggested by this shift in recruiting, it should be noted that when Japanese companies complain of a "shortage of labor" they usually are in fact complaining that middle school graduates—the least costly in terms of wages and most accommodating in terms of starting jobs—are diminishing sharply in numbers as the educational level of the whole society moves sharply upward.

In terms of female recruits to the work force, the proportion recruited from universities remained low—4 percent in 1956, and only 3 percent in 1966. This reflects the inability of the Japanese company to use women in jobs of any significance and the unattractiveness of corporate employment to well-educated women in Japan. It is extremely difficult to integrate a college-trained woman into a system in which she is no more than a drawer of tea and hewer of paper. Even female recruits, however, reflect the steadily increasing emphasis on education, in that more than three-quarters of the new female entrants to these work forces in 1966 were higher school graduates compared with 56 percent in 1956.

Compensation of Employees

A further test of change in Japanese organization methods is that of compensation. Japanese compensation has three main components. The first is wage or salary, the second a bonus paid semiannually and to a degree dependent on corporate results, and the third a wide range of fringe benefits and perquisites. The reports of the twenty-five companies studied regarding compensation in 1956 and 1966 are summarized in Exhibit 9.

Exhibit 9

ANNUAL COMPENSATION, 1956 AND 1966 PER INDIVIDUAL
(Average in $ equivalent)

	1956			1966			
	Salary or Wages ($)	Bonus ($)	Total ($)	Salary or Wages ($)	Bonus ($)	Total ($)	Increase 1966 over 1956 (%)
Top management	5,328	2,694	8,022	11,496	6,994	18,490	130
Middle management	2,088	1,188	3,276	3,408	2,466	5,874	79
Male employees	804	302	1,106	1,524	646	2,170	96
Female employees	425	142	567	840	320	1,160	106
Temporary workers	396	70	466	756	262	1,018	118

The average cash compensation in 1966 of the twenty or so men who direct each of these large companies was reported to be about $18,500 annually. Slightly more than a third of this was in the form of bonus payments, with base salaries averaging slightly less than $1,000 monthly. Executive compensation was up substantially from the $8,000 a year level of 1956, still very low indeed by Western standards. This group includes, of course, the board chairmen, presidents, and managing directors of large companies. Even at the $18,500 level, executive compensation had increased more rapidly over the decade than was the case with other categories of company employees.

Overall, compensation for employees of these companies roughly doubled in the decade. Within each of the employee groups, there is, of course, wide variation in compensation depending on length of service and level of schooling. The level of starting compensation is a function of educational background, and base compensation increases in direct relation to length of service. These two factors combine in the case of female and temporary employees whose educational level and length of service is low to make for very low levels of compensation, only slightly above $1,000 annually. Average annual compensation for male employees was about twice that of female employees, $2,170. The average compensation of middle management personnel increased less rapidly than that of the other groups, to just under $6,000 per year. This is no doubt due to the build-up in size of the middle management group, with the result that average length of service decreased over the decade for the group.

Fringe Benefits and Allowances

In addition to base salary or wages and bonus payments, employees of Japanese companies receive a variety of fringe benefits and perquisites. For senior officers of a publicly held company, these may include car and driver, company-owned housing and substantial expense accounts. For clerical employees and laborers, a range of special allowances is paid, housing or housing allowances may be provided, and the company in addition may provide such perquisites as company stores for discount purchases and mountain and seaside vacation facilities. The foreign observer of Japan, taken aback at low salary levels and impressed by the company hospitality offered him, is apt to exaggerate considerably the magnitude of these fringe benefits and their impact on the individual employee's income. Putting closely-held or family-owned companies to one side as a special case (as indeed they are also in the West), the increment to income of the employee and his family of a large company of these benefits is minor except in the case of housing.

In this survey, two elements of these fringe benefits were examined: company-owned housing and special allowances. The proportion of employees provided company-owned housing in 1966 was 21 percent for top management, 44 percent for middle management, 34 percent for male employees and 8 percent for female employees. In sum, perhaps one-third of company employees are provided company housing. The proportion in company housing was down slightly for all categories of employees from 1956.

This housing is rented to the employee at nominal rental amounts, and its quality depends on rank in the company. As a man is promoted, he will successively move to larger and more attractive housing. The quality is often not high. In one discussion comparing U.S. and Japanese salaries, a young Japanese executive was reminded that he paid virtually nothing for his housing and replied that he was paying precisely what it was worth. However, in housing-short Japan, where rentals can be very high indeed, provision of company housing is a substantial increment to real income.

The low proportion of senior executives in company housing probably does not entirely reflect their real housing benefits. Several companies included in this study have made it possible for executives to buy company houses at book value (well below market value) and finance the purchase by a loan from the company against their retirement allowance. The capital gain to the individual under this arrangement is considerable.

The range of allowances paid to employees below the management level is shown in Exhibit 10. The seventeen allowances listed are not exhaustive, but are those most commonly offered employees. Five allowances are paid by virtually every company included in this study. Three of these are normal international practice—special pay for holiday, overtime or night work. One company only does not pay a special allowance for overtime or night work; this is a manufacturer that put its entire work force on a salary basis in 1965. Two of these generally paid allowances are more special to Japan: the payment of part or all of commutation expenses which is a tax deductible expense item for Japanese companies, and the payment of a family allowance, intended to partly compensate the employee for the additional costs of maintaining a family (these payments are small).

Among the other allowances listed in Exhibit 10, a shift in emphasis should be noted. Allowances for age and length of service declined in frequency from 1956 to 1966, while allowances for position, job classification (*shokumukyu*) and "special work" increased in incidence. This reflects an effort on the

Exhibit 10

COMPANIES PAYING SPECIAL WORKER ALLOWANCES,
1956 AND 1966

Allowance	Number of Companies 1966	Number of Companies 1956
Commutation	25	22
Holiday work	25	24
Family	24	23
Overtime	24	24
Night work	24	22
Position	19	17
Job classification	17	9
Dangerous work	14	12
Housing allowance	13	8
Cold district	13	11
Length of service	11	15
Age	10	12
Vacation	10	11
Area	9	10
Attendance	7	9
Efficiency	6	8
Remote area	4	3

part of many companies to move toward compensation based on job and output and away from compensation based on age and education. Eight companies introduced a job classification allowance in the decade, so that by 1966 most included a job classification allowance in total compensation. This change should be reviewed with some caution, however. In at least some of these companies the job classifications established were little more than seniority categories under another name.

To put this matter of extensive allowances in perspective, the sums involved need to be noted. They are small. Average allowance payments in 1956 for male employees were about a 20 percent increment to base wages or $160 for the year. In 1966, the ratio to base wages had declined to about 18 percent, or a total allowance payment of about $276 for the year. This represented a 12 to 13 percent increase in total cash compensation (wages plus bonus). For female employees, allowances represented an increment to base wages in both 1956 and 1966 of about 10 percent, or an addition to cash compensation of 7 to 8 percent. In sum, then, a wide variety of types of allowances, many paternalistic in nature, continued, and were paid in about the same proportion at the end of the ten-year period as in 1956.

Leaving the Japanese Company

A critical test of the degree and kind of change in organization methods in Japan is the movement of employees out of companies. The lifetime employment concept assumes that the individual employee will not quit the company and that the company will not lay off or discharge the employee. While such a system could hardly exist in its pure form, it has been an accurate way to describe the normative behavior of employers and employees in Japan. Indeed, this concept is a key to Japanese employment practices since many of the paternalistic features of employment are directly derived from this principle of an exchange of social obligation on the part of employee and employer.

The question of whether this basic principle is changing has been the subject of some controversy. Exhibit 11 summarizes the results of a comparison of exit rates and causes for the twenty-five companies for 1956 and 1966. The exit rate from companies, as a component of labor turnover rate, did not change appreciably in the decade, with the exception of female employees whose exit rate increased rather sharply. The proportion of management and of male employees who have left the company in the year was substantially the same. The proportion of female employees leaving these companies in the year increased from 9 percent to 15 percent, parallel to the increase in percentage recruited in the two years from 8 percent to 14 (see Exhibit 7).

Looking at the causes for leaving the work force, with the exception of discharge from the companies which is discussed further below, the pattern of causes changed little. Most management personnel retire for reasons of age. Some middle management personnel, and over half of male employees, retire for reasons of health, family needs (such as returning to agricultural work), and other personal reasons. (This category may include employees who leave for other work. To the extent that it does, the proportion seems not to have changed over the decade.) Almost all female employees leave for personal reasons, and in almost all cases this reason is marriage. By company rule earlier, and by continuing custom, women leave the industrial work force at or soon after marriage.

The category of "related companies" requires some comment. The retirement age in Japan for all but top management is usually 55 years. Since new employment at that age is difficult to obtain, retirement payments small, and social security benefits much smaller, retirement at so early an age causes a real hardship in many cases. One form of fringe benefit available to a favored employee is to position him in a senior position in a subsidiary or affiliated company where he can continue in full-time and fully compensated employment for some additional years. It is likely that most cases of exit to related companies are of this type.

Thus, the rate and causes of leaving the work force appear to have changed very little over this decade of rapid economic change—with one exception, and a critical one: discharge. From almost no cases of firings in 1956, discharge from the company appears in 1966 as a significant cause of exits from these companies. Of the 3 percent of middle management who left their companies, 5 percent were fired.

Exhibit 11

LEAVING THE COMPANY
(Average, 25 companies)

	Top Management 1956 1966		Middle Management 1956 1966		Male Employees 1956 1966		Female Employees 1956 1966	
Exits from work force as percent of total	2	2	5	3	3	4	9	15
Of which,								
retirement for age	100	100	67	56	40	36	1	2
retirement for voluntary reasons	0	0	27	25	56	54	99	97
move to job with related company	0	0	6	7	2	5	0	0
discharge	0	0	0	13	2	5	0	1

To put the proportions in perspective, these discharges totaled less than two-tenths of one percent of the 1966 work force. The numbers are tiny, by any measure. Yet, the question remains, does this indicate the beginnings of a real and basic change in the way in which the Japanese business organization operates? The answer is not entirely clear, but closer examination of the data suggested that a basic change had not yet taken place.

Of the discharges reported, totaling about 450 out of a total work force of 260,000, the majority were discharges from a single company. Almost all of the middle management and of the female employee cases and most of the male employee cases occurred in this one company. This company stated:

> The cases of discharge are the result of a rationalization of management, and while these employees were discharged, they were given assistance in finding other employment.

The company in question is a leader in an industry that is under severe pressure in Japan due to raw materials sourcing problems and uneconomic size of production units. As a result, this company was by a considerable margin the slowest growing of the twenty-five companies included in the study. Against an average increase in sales of more than four times of other companies studied, its sales increased in dollar value only about 70 percent in the ten years. What is referred to by this company as "rationalization of management" in justifying its dismissal of employees rather clearly was a drastic surgery carried out in 1966 aimed at saving an organization in deep trouble.

This case suggests that the basic rules of lifetime commitment remained in force to about the same extent as a decade earlier, but that under extreme stress a kind of spasm-reaction can take place in a company during which the rule is temporarily waived to deal with severe crisis. It is, of course, implicit in the explanation given by the company in question that these cases of discharge were temporary deviations from the norm of corporate policy.

It will be recalled that one of these twenty-five companies deviated from normal practice and recruited a number of middle management personnel from the outside labor market. This was, by a good margin, the fastest-growing company in this group. Again, in terms of discharge—the other extreme form of deviation from normal practice—it is the slowest-growing company that provides the instance of exceptional behavior.

Some Conclusions

In spite of the phenomenal character and the rapidity of the transformation of Japan, it has not been accompanied by such a revolutionary break with the traditions and customs of the past as was caused by the development of industry in some Western countries. Here it is only necessary to emphasize once more the importance of taking the family system into account in examining the problems of industrial Japan. . . . Out of this influence arises a fundamental problem for the future of industrial organization in Japan.

This problem may be stated as being whether the future industrial organization of Japan is to be evolved in conflict between the traditional influences and ideas—especially the family system—and the new ideas and institutions which in Japan as in most other countries have accompanied the growth of industry, or whether means can be developed of integrating the new institutions in the traditional Japanese social organization.

This statement of degree and rate of change in Japanese organizations was published over a generation ago, in 1933.[1]

The issue has not changed since the 1930's. This study of the 1956–1966 period indicates again the durability of Japan's approach to industrial organization. There has been a general

---

[1]*Industrial Labour in Japan.* Studies and Reports, Series A (Industrial Relations) No. 37, Geneva: International Labour Office, 1933, p. 370.

tendency to assume that Japanese companies are changing in their methods of organization. This data does not encourage that view. No doubt Japanese society, like any other, is changing and will continue to change, and no doubt its institutions—companies, schools, families and the like—will be components of that change. But it seems quite clear that the change will be slow and continuous, and little evident in so short a period as ten years. Societies do not change so quickly as that in their fundamentals, however much the surface may reflect change.

As the 1933 study concluded:

> It would be hazardous to attempt to forecast the probable lines of development of Japanese industrial organization.[1]

It is by no means clear that change, as it may occur, will be soon, or toward the Western model.

---

[1]*Ibid.*, p. 371.

INDEX

INDEX